WILDCOOK

ceps, shrubs & rock 'n' roll

WILDCOOK

ceps, shrubs & rock 'n' roll

Garry Eveleigh

Food by James Golding
Foreword by Robin Hutson

Published by Zsazseva Publishing
www.zsazseva.com

ISBN: 978-0-956-5771-9-1

British Library Cataloguing-in-Publication Data: A catalogue record for this book is available from the British Library.

Concept, art direction, compilation & edit by Penny Ericson assisted by Mary Anne Martin and Simon Hawkins
Designed by Hilite Design & Reprographics
Photographs by Matt Dunkinson Photography & Video Production
Illustrations by Gigi Eveleigh
Managed and manufactured by Jellyfish Print Solutions, Swanmore, Hampshire UK

Printed and bound in the United Kingdom

Stocks from sustainable sources

FSC

Other photo credits:

Angel Publicity: page 7 • Courtesy of Repertoire Food & Design, *Chemo Cookery Club*: page 13; page 182; page 184 – 'mayonnaise'; pages 198 – 189 • Courtesy of Repertoire Food & Design, *Meats, Eats, Drinks & Leaves*: page 50 • Jeremy Coombs: pages 28-29; pages 56-59; page 68; page 69 –' sea beet', 2 right hand images; page 77; page 159 – right photo; page 160; pages 164-167; page 175; page 187 – 'wild sorrel' • John at foragelondon.co.uk: pages 86-87; pages 92 – 93; page 97 – 'oyster mushrooms on tree', right; page 102; page 107 • Penny Ericson: page 10; page 20; pages 88-89; page 97 – 'oyster mushrooms on moss', left; pages 129-130; page 150 – left photo; page 184 – 'fresh pasta'; page 185 – sorrel vinegar • Kate Gillman: page 91; page 109 – 'Anna & bunny', centre; page 103 • Simon Hawkins: page 10 • Emma Moore: page 6; page 63; page 112 • Various photographers under Shutterstock licence agreement: page 33 – brown shrimp on plate, Food pictures; page 45 – left photo, razor shells, MAMZ images; page 106, Daniel Peter Ronneberg; page 112, Aleksandar Milutinovic; page 113, Michaelpuche; page 120, Hector Ruiz Villar; page 121 – left photo, Martin Fowler, right photo, SIA Yasu; page 138, Neil Webster; page 139, Firma V; page 143, Linda George; page 147 – left photo, Martin Fowler, right photo, Emi; page 193, Andrew Koturanov.

ACKNOWLEDGEMENTS

FROM GARRY

Over the years many friends have said to me, 'You should write a book', so after much badgering and over half a decade later it's time to say thank-you.

A big thanks to Caroline for being gorgeous, wonderful, perfect and my saviour in many ways.

Thanks to Genevieve *Gigi*, Piers, Kate and Zoe for just being the best kids on the planet and a special thank-you to my youngest daughter Gigi for her stunning sketches and illustrations throughout the book and much more, you're a very talented young lady, love you sweetie xxx, dad.

Thanks to Jeremy and Nancy Coombs and the boys for joining me on many walks, taking some great photographs and tasting or rather devouring almost everything I cooked in those early days. Also, to Tim and Kate Gillman for joining me year-on-year at *THE PIG*. Their delightful daughter Anna is featured on page 107.

For some invaluable lessons in English, a big thank-you to my cousin David Brushett. As my school reports said, *'could do better.'* Thanks David.

A huge thanks to Robin Hutson for his trust and for giving me the chance to pass on my crazy foraging knowledge to so many guests at his fabulous hotels, *Lime Wood* and *THE PIG* and for his very kind words in the foreword. To each and every member of staff at *Lime Wood* and *THE PIG*, for always being so courteous, kind and very welcoming every time I walk through the door, thank-you all.

Thank you so much to Heather at *HHB Agency*, for believing in me and giving me the confidence to write.

Thanks to Mark Hix for his anecdotes and words of wisdom and for allowing me to entertain people at *Food Rocks* in Lyme Regis for the last few years.

Thanks to Dave at Hilite Design for his skill and just the right touch in putting the whole book together, Sam at Jellyfish for her wizardry in the dark art of print management and for his amazing photography, I have to thank Matt Dunkinson. Over the years, his vision of my foraging world has been absolutely spot on. *Cheers Matt!*

An enormous thank-you to Penny Ericson and her husband Simon Hawkins, for making the whole thing come together. *Let's rock 'n roll again!*

A very special thank-you to James Golding for his fantastic recipes that make the book come alive and hopefully will inspire many readers to *'go wild!'*

My last and biggest thanks goes to my great friends, Tony and Mary Anne Martin. They have ridden the crest of the wave with me from start to finish and have had a massive input in so many ways. Thank-you both for eating kilos and kilos of wild mushrooms, plants, scallops and superb fresh fish along the way – see you both soon.

ACKNOWLEDGEMENTS FROM JAMES

I've had a wonderful time working on this book. I'm especially delighted that my friend Garry's vast knowledge and experience can be shared. So in the first instance, thanks Garry for including me in your magical world of wild food.

It's a great job being a chef but it's not as easy as it appears and there are so many people that have nurtured and supported me along the way.

For my family, especially my parents, Richard & Sue and Mary & Bruce, thanks for sticking with me; dad for spending all those years teaching me about foraging and doing your chef course; mum for all your pasta making & giving me that first job plucking pheasants (no really!) and all of you for your endless support through all the long hours, mood swings, grueling training and restaurants home and abroad. I couldn't have done it without the great foundation you gave me and the knowledge that home was never far away.

To 'Chef', aka David Boland & Jenny Brett at *Bournemouth College,* spec chef programme. Thank-you for seeing something in me all those years ago, sending me to *The Savoy* and pushing me on, it paid off!

I'd like to pay my respects and say a special thanks to thanks my *Nonna* Maria for smuggling back jars of anchovies in her handbag on the plane from Italy to eat in the car on the way home! And Nanny Doris for introducing me to Good Friday homemade skate & chips and her most incredible chicken liver pâté!

Finally, my amazing wife Ericka, and our kids Rex & Rio, you are simply a wonderful family and my complete pride and joy!

FOREWORD

A few years ago I was developing our *PIG* restaurant concept of serving guests only home grown and locally sourced food. I envisaged giving our guests a 'live' food experience, picking their own veg from our kitchen garden or gathering that morning's harvest of freshly laid eggs from our hens. Then I thought you can't get more 'live' than spending a morning rustling through a forest collecting a basket of wild mushrooms, garlic and chestnuts or strolling the beach for sea vegetables and shellfish then watching a chef create a dish with your bounty. The trick is you have to know what you're looking for and where to find it.

To test the idea, we invited a few of the UK's most experienced and clever chefs to participate in a friendly competition – a kind of rustic *Masterchef* skills test. Each chef had to create a dish using fresh foraged ingredients. That's when I first met Garry Eveleigh. He presented the chefs with baskets, trollies and buckets filled with edible plants and shellfish that he'd foraged that morning and then left them to get on with it. These ingredients could not have been fresher, more local or seasonal!

To go for a walk with Garry is to put your senses in hyper-drive. By the time you've spotted a patch of ramson, he's delicately picked and cleaned the finest leaves and flowers leaving the bed looking as fresh as it ever was and in the meantime, he's probably caught a rare glimpse of a kingfisher and foraged a basket of wild chanterelles and while your eyes are still adjusting to the light, he's likely plucked half a dozen beautiful, edible flowers for you to sample.

Garry's infectious enthusiasm ensures hours on end disappear without noticing. He appears to get as much pleasure in sharing his vast knowledge and respect for nature as actually gathering produce.

Whilst he is clearly a beneficiary of his own foraging, Garry also thinks of himself as the custodian of his 'wild patch' of forest and coastline – a patch he has tended and cared for over decades.

The provenance of locally sourced food and the strong 'garden to plate' philosophy we operate in our restaurants is at the heart of everything we do. This concept is only further enhanced by our chefs and working closely with Garry. On so many occasions I see Garry at the back door of one of our kitchens with a crowd of beaming chefs around him having just delivered yet another previously unidentified treasure. Then, minutes later finding the same treasure enhancing a brand new dish on the menu. Garry is the epitome of local sourcing. Happy foraging!

Robin Hutson
THE PIG & Lime Wood Hotels

IN MEMORY

This book is dedicated to the memories of my dear old mum, Mary Irene and my big bro Terry, who slipped away in the night when we were teenagers. Sadly, mother couldn't hang around long enough to see the finished book either. She was nothing other than wonderful and I can picture her now saying to me, *'If you keep bringing this stuff home, you'd better learn how to cook.'* Her smiley face and words of wisdom inspired me from the tender age of nine.

So now they're walking, hand in hand.
Across a hill, along the sand.
Both have waited, so many years.
Their hearts have wept, a million tears.
So please don't weep, upon this day.
Are words I hear, my Mother say.
Be proud, be happy, remember this.
Upon his cheek, she placed my kiss.

Love you always.
Garry

CONTENTS

Notes to our readers   10

Becoming the Wildcook   16

When Garry met James   21

When James met Garry   23

Gathering shellfish   24

On the beach   52

The forest floor & more   86

Hedgerow harvest   124

Wild salad   154

Basics & extras   188

Glossary of terms   198

Conversion chart   200

James' preferred suppliers   202

Index   203

NOTES TO OUR READERS

Editor's notes

It's a delight to live in the south of England next to the New Forest and Garry has made what's on my doorstep come alive – times ten! Creating this book with him has filled me with wonder. I've particularly enjoyed going out on walks in the forest, hedgerows and on the foreshore soaking up Garry's knowledge of the outdoors and how to use its bounty in the kitchen. The experience has been truly second to none.

Garry's enthusiasm and boundless energy are infectious. I don't even look at my garden in the same way and find myself picking dandelions and little daisies before I mow the lawn! Thank-you Garry for inviting me into Mother Nature's larder and sharing time with me in her kitchen. I hope you enjoy using this book as an informative introduction and guide to foraging and equally as culinary adventure with wild food.

If you're interested in learning more about Garry and James' foraging and wild food we'd love to hear from you at www.wildcook.co.uk.

Happy hunting and bon appetite!

On Garry's foraging

Garry has spent his entire life dedicated to the New Forest and surrounding areas where he grew up and still lives. While everything in this book applies around the UK and in other regions, his perspective is specific to his local area and there may be environmental variations that cause changes in things like the timing of picking seasons or the abundance of a particular fruit. There will also be rules and bylaws specific to different regions so we urge you to have a full understanding of these before you set out.

In everything that Garry does as a hunter-gatherer, he follows a few golden rules that respect and protect the environment, assure personal and public safety and operate within the laws and bylaws of the UK. Here are a few guidelines he conveys before he sets out on any walk or foraging expedition. They should always be adhered to:

Safety

Accurate advice on tide tables and shellfish orders & details for *Local Harbour Authority or Sea Fisheries District Office.*

Checking tide times

Always check tide times before venturing out on any foreshore. Tide times in the UK vary around the coast depending on the position of the moon, sun and various other influences. Using tide tables, generated from tidal prediction data, it is possible to see where and when a high tide will occur on any date at a given location. For accurate information visit www.tidetimes.org.uk.

Positive identification

In his narrative, Garry often refers to 'the all important identification rule' – if you aren't 100% sure what it is don't pick it and certainly don't eat it! Please apply this especially to mushroom gathering – a mistake could be more than a little costly.

On James' recipes & food

I've worked with a lot of chefs over the years and James Golding is right at the top of my list. Like Garry, he's a complete one off! What makes him so unique is the way he effortlessly combines his sophisticated background and training in French and classic cuisine with his straightforward and honest approach to cooking. His love of wild food has always been with him and it shows. If you've had the pleasure of dining in any of his restaurants you'll know what I mean and if you haven't I recommend it take priority on your bucket list.

James makes food more than enjoyable – he makes it fun and fills any food experience with energy. Whether he's inventing new recipes for his *A Pinch of Salt* charcuterie, mentoring and training rising new chefs or 'rattling pans' in one of *THE PIG's* kitchens, it's done with equal skill, authenticity and enthusiasm.

The recipes James presents in *Wildcook* just flick the tip of the iceberg and at the same time open up endless possibilities. Once you've tried one recipe you're set to invent a myriad of your own. I hope you enjoy them as much as I do.

If there are any instances where a process seems unclear or missing, I apologise – any errors and omissions are mine. All of the dishes presented have been tested, prepared and photographed in a domestic kitchen but James, like many chefs, works to his own culinary shorthand and sometimes at a speed that many would find bewildering. If I've missed something, it might be that he changed it on the spot or he simply forgot to tell me. (Extracting accurate recipes out of any chef takes some doing!)

When we were photographing the food for *Wildcook*, a few of the mushrooms were out of season so we substituted other, available wild mushrooms or used varieties that Garry had picked and dried the previous season. These variations have been footnoted and we hope it illustrates that the recipes are flexible and open to your personal interpretation. If you can't get an ingredient use your creativity.

In the back of the book there is a section called *Basics & extras* that sets out recipes and processes that underpin James' dishes such as court bouillon and making fresh pasta. We've also included a few of Garry's fast and fresh favourites.

I've tried to be consistent from recipe to recipe but chefs simply don't work that way and James is no exception. Here is the guidance we gave to our fabulous friends that tested and gave feedback on the recipes:

A word on eggs

Use large free-range and organic if there isn't a specific instruction. Egg yolks are measured in 2 ways, by quantity (ie 3 yolks) and also in grams. 1 large free-range yolk = 25 g on average. The reason for the two styles is that many chefs use liquid pasteurised yolks. The measurements are accurate and they are safer from a health and safety perspective. If you're pregnant or in a vulnerable health group, avoid raw or partially cooked eggs.

A word on wine, spirits & the use of alcohol

Some of James' recipes include alcohol as an ingredient. It's used to add and enhance flavour, for example, in a marinade or flambé or as an aperitif to 'tingle the taste buds'. The intention is to add to the enjoyment of food and enhance flavour. When heated, alcohol evaporates but the flavour remains. In every instance the recipes can be followed without the use of alcohol. Substitutes can be used, for example using a juniper berry infusion to replace gin. I leave it to you, the cook, to choose.

Cleaning and filleting roundfish

Trim off the fins with kitchen scissors. Under running water, grip the fish by the tail and scrape it from the tail toward the head with a fish scaler or blunt knife. Next, slit open the belly from the anal fin to the head. Pull out the guts and wash until clean then trim the edges. If the fish is large, pull open the gill flaps and cut away the gills at the back of the head and under the mouth.

To fillet the fish, use either a filleting knife or a knife with a flexible blade. Lay the fish on a board with its back toward you, cut around the back of the head, through the flesh of the fillet and down the backbone. Turn the knife toward the tail and beginning just behind the head, carefully start to cut the fillet away from the bones, down toward the belly. Once you have loosened enough flesh to get the whole blade under the fillet, rest your free hand on top of the fish and cut away the fillet in one steady, clean sweep keeping the blade as close to the bones as possible. Turn the fish over and repeat on the other side. Remove any pin-bones with a pair of tweezers.

Cleaning shellfish

Nothing ruins a bowl of clams, mussels, or cockles like a mouthful of grit. Purge and clean your shellfish properly and leave the sand where it should be, on the beach. Store bought shellfish is usually pre-cleaned, even so, you should still carefully clean and check each piece before cooking. After gathering a feed the best thing to do is leave the shellfish to soak in fresh seawater in a cool, dark place for 24 hours. When ready to serve, rinse the shellfish under running water to remove loose sediment, discarding any with broken shells. Healthy shellfish will close their shells when tapped so discard any that don't. Next transfer to a pot of fresh seawater or cold salted water and refrigerate for 30 minutes, stirring occasionally. When ready to cook, lift the shellfish out of the water by hand so you can feel for remaining sediment and for mussels pinch off the beards. When serving, spoon out if using the liquor, pass through a fine sieve to remove any last grit released during cooking.

Cooking times

Timings are given as a guideline and in most cases with a description of the finished article. We rely on you, the cook, to use your judgment.

Dehydrating vegetables

The three basic methods are: sun, oven and electric dehydration. Sun drying can be tricky in many climates as you need at least 3 days of temperatures over 35°C (100°F). Oven drying works well if you have an oven that can maintain a temperature below 95°C (200°F – very cool) and air circulation is critical. We recommend using an electric dehydrator and follow the manufacturer's temperature guidance.

You will know your food is dried when you touch it. It is leathery with no pockets of moisture. If you are testing fruit, you can tear a piece in half. If you see moisture beads along the tear, it is not dry enough. Meat should be tough, but shouldn't snap apart. Vegetables should also be tough but can also be crisp. Dried produce must be completely moisture free and airtight. Sterilised canning jars and plastic freezer bags are good for this and should be kept in a cool, dark, dry place.

Edible flowers

Here are a few suggestions of flowers that are commonly available in the wild and many can be found in your garden:
daisies
dandelion
forget-me-not
honesty
mallow
marigold
ramson
sea campion
three-cornered garlic

Measurements & quantities

Some measures are precise to the extreme, while others are a bit more 'freestyle' so taste your food as you work to balance flavours.

Oven temperatures

I've used settings for conventional ovens. Decrease the temperature by 15°C if you are using a fan-assisted oven. Individual ovens can vary by as much as 10°C and possibly more when transferring from a commercial to domestic kitchen. Get to know your oven. The best gauge is a thermometer.

Seasoning

In this book seasoning has been kept simple. The salt, unless otherwise indicated is Maldon salt (a high quality sea salt). White pepper has been used during cooking processes and fresh black pepper as a flavour to finished dishes. Other seasonings are clearly indicated in the recipes but the measurements are approximate due to variations in ingredients and personal taste. We leave it to you, the cook, to find your own balance.

Special equipment

We've maintained that each dish is home kitchen friendly. Here are a few bits of kit that are 'nice to have' but not essential. Where we've specified special or professional equipment we have also offered alternative preparation methods. If you decide that wild cooking is the thing for you consider investing in: a dehydrator, ice cream maker, fine muslin straining cloths and plenty of kilner or canning jars.

Sterilising jars & lids

Jars should be made from glass and free of any chips or cracks. Preserving or canning jars are topped with a glass, plastic or metal lid, which has a rubber seal. Two-piece lids are best for canning, as they vacuum-seal when processed. To sterilise, wash jars, lids and a pair of tongs with hot, soapy water then boil the jars and lids in a large saucepan, covered with water for 15 minutes. Use tongs when handling the sterilised jars and lids. As a rule, hot preserves go into hot jars and cold preserves go into cold jars. All items used in the process of making jams, jellies and preserves must be clean. This includes any towels used, and especially your hands.

BECOMING THE WILDCOOK

The Mole had been working very hard all the morning, spring-cleaning his little home. First with brooms, then with dusters; then on ladders and steps and chairs, with a brush and a pail of whitewash; till he had dust in his throat and eyes, and splashes of whitewash all over his black fur, and an aching back and weary arms. Spring was moving in the air above and in the earth below and around him, penetrating even his dark and lowly little house with its spirit of divine discontent and longing.

Kenneth Graham, *The Wind in the Willows*

Some things in life simply happen. There's no great intention, no carefully considered result and certainly no plan. Perhaps there is a bit of serendipity.

My interest in nature began at a tender age. I can't say exactly when, but I remember vividly while still attending junior school convincing my dear old mum that I could walk a brisk two miles to school on my own. The route took me along quiet country lanes and by great fortune past an irresistible fishing spot, hmm. My route should have taken just over half an hour but I was an inquisitive lad and there were things to see, the world to watch and so much to do. I'll never forget my first close encounter with a wild animal; well, don't get too excited it wasn't exactly a tiger!

It was a gorgeous spring morning. I was strolling along gazing about and listening to the wondrous sounds of nature when my eye caught a strange movement coming from some freshly dug soil. A large embankment was aglow with a stunning array of primroses, violets and wood anemones and the earth was moving...quite literally.

I approached very quietly. Something was churning fresh soil onto the bank. With curious abandon I didn't hesitate to investigate. My nose was within inches of the growing earthwork when a ginormous black mole with huge pink feet burst from the oozing mound of soil. I froze and stared in utter amazement. So did he! Being a fan of *The Wind in the Willows*, I half-expected my new acquaintance to wish me, '*Good morning!*' My new mole friend sniffed the air intently; likely got one whiff of me, then beat a hasty retreat back from where he'd come. I was blown away.

A little further on from Mr Mole's mound at the bottom of the hill flowed the Wainsford River. There was a pool on the left side of the bridge that was always good to catch a brown trout or two. Yellow wagtails bobbed their grey and yellow tails while catching insects and it was always a bonus hearing the shrill two-tone whistle of an electric-blue kingfisher flashing his way downstream. You could always hear them before you could see them, but if I was lucky I'd catch a glimpse.

On the other side of the bridge the strong current of winter floods had pushed up a huge shingle bank to create an island with the river flowing down either side. It was perfect...so off with my school shoes and socks and I quickly paddled to the island. On the downstream side of my newly conquered kingdom I quickly got to work scraping out my very own holding pool leaving a trickle of water to feed into the stirred up muddy water. My junior school engineering skills paid off and my

pool was soon crystal clear. Now all I needed was to put something in it. The moving water on either side of my shingle island was perfect for catching lamprey. These eel-like primitive vertebrates have a green to blue back with a silvery-white belly. They don't have a jaw or bones, instead a thorny row of teeth inside their circular sucking mouth and a spine of cartilage. To catch my quarry I had to wade upstream in the freezing water. The slippery customers were easy prey as they anchored themselves by suction to the stones on the riverbed; so by using both hands I swiftly scooped a handful of shingle with a few lamprey attached and bingo, they were in my holding pool. My feet turned bright red and numb and a dozen lampreys were looking for the exit from my freshwater aquarium. I was spellbound.

I arrived at school sometime around mid-morning and was made to stand in the corner for being late. 'Hah, perfect,' I thought; it gave me time to reminisce about my encounter with Mr Mole and relive my lamprey gathering!

My relationship with nature quickly grew from simple curiosity to complete fascination. I learned everything I could on a simple 'need to know' basis. Mother Nature was by far my favourite teacher and by the age of just twelve I knew every bird and its song, the names of every wild flower, bunches of which I would regularly pick for my mum and I had discovered my favourite patches for picking field mushrooms. I was even earning my keep! By picking a bucketful of wild watercress I earned sixpence a week. Mum would make fresh cheese and watercress sandwiches to sell in our pub and my cut was a penny per sandwich. There I was - twelve years old earning pocket money by doing what came naturally. I suppose it was my first big lesson in life and it felt like it couldn't get any better!

My enthusiasm continued and my childhood playground soon expanded. The marshes and estuary were just a short bicycle ride away and at low tide I could often be found digging ragworms that were used as fishing bait for catching flounder and sea bass. I would always keep my eyes peeled for telltale squirts of water from cockles living just below the mud's surface or gather a feed of winkles that were abundant. During the spring black-headed gull's eggs could be gathered from the saltgrass marshes that were cut off by each incoming tide and marsh samphire was easy pickings. I would never go home with an empty bucket and I'm still the same today. Some things never change.

At sixteen I became really mobile – I acquired my first motorbike. Up to this point the New Forest had been a destination for family picnics. Now it was just up the road for me. The wildlife was and still is amazing and over the last forty-five years I've explored virtually every acre of ancient woodland in search of wild mushrooms and other edible delights and along the way I have filled my mind with so much natural history of the region and its inhabitants. It still holds me in wonder and I'm still learning.

I can honestly say that I know the best bits of the forest like the back of my hand. Of the two thousand or more varieties of fungi that grow in the New Forest my personal picking list is whittled

down to just twenty or so and my top ten are the most delicious mushrooms that money simply can't buy.

Today, there are sections of woodland where large areas of mycelium lay hidden beneath the forest floor that produce fruiting bodies when conditions are perfect. These areas have grown and spread to three times the size, and larger, from when I first started gathering these wild delicacies all those years ago. I think this is proof in itself that the rumours of over-picking are a myth and that respect for nature and careful management is essential.

For more than five decades the New Forest, its outlying regions and foreshores have been my home, livelihood and wonderland. In all those years I've never tired of it and to this day, every time I drive my old school route, I still re-live my first encounter with Mr Mole and look to see if my shale island in the Wainsford River is still buffeting the chilly currents.

Happy Fathers Day 2013

the stars are all
my friends

till the night time
ends, but I know I'm
not alone, when I'm
here, on my own, isn't
that a wonder, when your
alone, your not alone
not really
alone ...

Robin Williams as Peter Pan in the film *Hook*

WHEN GARRY MET JAMES

In 2010 I was offered an opportunity that I couldn't refuse. It would give me the chance to share my wealth of self-taught knowledge about the New Forest and surrounding areas to visitors. I became the foraging guide for the exclusive *Lime Wood Group* of hotels. To kick things off, in the spring of that year I was asked to 'bring a couple of baskets of foraged ingredients' for a photo shoot with the chefs. 'A couple of baskets they said?' It was time to use my foraging know-how to produce a mighty impressive and tasty trove. I was on it!

As temperatures rise in the spring, wild edible plants thrive in the damp soil. There was a bounty to choose from and I quite literally filled the back of my estate car with as many varieties of wild goodies as I could fit, all freshly picked that morning and placed in buckets of water to keep fresh.

On arrival at the hotel I grabbed one of the pretty wicker trolleys that the porters use for transporting guests' luggage. I then set to work creating a mind-blowing display of delicious, edible greens and flowers. There I had it; a perfect cartload of totally wild, freshly gathered and completely free ingredients.

I made my way to the rear terrace of the hotel where the photo shoot would take place and as my overflowing cartload and I made our entrance we were greeted with, 'What's all that?' I simply replied, 'That's all edible, hah.' That was my first encounter with chef James Golding. He was blown away.

Little did I know that as a youngster his father had taken him foraging and in that instant I had transported him back to his youth. His enthusiasm was bubbling over. James was tearing off fragments of plants and nibbling at them asking, 'What's this one? Where did you pick this? How did you learn all this stuff?'

It was clear that we had a lot to talk about. I explained to James how I'd become a hunter-gatherer and that it had all stemmed from my lifelong curiosity of edible wild food and my own interest in cooking that had been with me since childhood. If something from the wild was edible I had a compulsion to learn all about it. I could tell that James' mind was in overdrive. I'd taken him back to his youth and he was buzzing with excitement. My display of tastes, textures, colours and flavour combinations were giving James some truly inspirational and great ideas.

As it turned out, this wasn't just a casual meeting; we were destined to become friends for life. Years on I'm still bringing wild edible goodies into James' kitchens and I still manage to surprise him every once in a while! It's a delight to take visitors into the New Forest to share a few of its secrets and return a few hours later with laden baskets for the chefs to cook a culinary delight for our guests. Sometimes you make your luck and once in a while there's a generous dollop of serendipity to finish the dish!

Happy foraging!

WHEN JAMES MET GARRY

I started working in professional kitchens when I was 16 and while still a student at the *Académie de Culinaire de France*, I began working my way up the ranks at London's *Savoy Hotel*. I've been privileged to learn under some of the finest chefs in the world and work in some of the finest restaurants and hotels in the UK and the US but my real love for food began in the New Forest when I was a young boy. My dad loved the outdoors and every weekend would take me and my brother into the forest to gather mushrooms or we could be found gathering blackberries, sloes or any number of wild ingredients to take home and whip into an adventurous treat. Back then I had little concept of how special the place I grew up was or how formative weekends foraging with my dad would be.

A few years ago I was given the opportunity to bring my international experience home to where my culinary heart beats. I had spent several years in the US as head chef at New York's *Soho House*. It was a great place to cook. The open, easy style of dining in America mixed with my formal French training started to define my style creating simple and elegant food that didn't take itself too seriously. As time went on the quality of individual ingredients became increasingly important and I was constantly on the lookout for the freshest local ingredients I could find. I still get a real buzz out of the challenge of being presented with fresh seasonal ingredients. It's like being a painter that's given a different palate of paint everyday.

A new hotel group based in the New Forest called *THE PIG* was about to be formed and I was to become its head chef. The concept was perfect – a lovely

country house was the setting to build a 'second to none' kitchen garden that allowed guests to see ingredients they'd be eating, growing in front of them then the rest sourced within a 25-mile radius. It was perfect, so I packed up my lovely wife and new baby and brought them home. I had come full circle...and then it got even better.

I was asked to take part in an event at our sister hotel *Lime Wood*. A group of chefs were going to meet a local forager. Using his ingredients and our creativity we were to create dishes that could really celebrate local cuisine. That's when it happened. I arrived at the hotel, strolled around the back to the kitchen entrance and saw basket upon basket upon bucket of freshly picked greens, flowers, berries – I didn't know the names of half of what I was looking at but I did know I wanted it all in my kitchen! I started asking Garry questions and in his easy way he started me down the path of using wild food in my daily menus.

Several years on our common love of nature and wild food has grown into a lasting friendship. The chefs at *THE PIG in the Forest* delight in the challenges they're presented with when Garry and our foraging guests turn up with their baskets and every so often he's still able to surprise me with a new edible morsel.

It's been a real pleasure sharing my ideas in this book about how easy and delicious wild food can be and a day out with Garry turns nature into an amazing grocery store!

Enjoy!

cockles and clams

Contents

ROCK LIMPET
DEVILLED ROCK LIMPETS

BROWN SHRIMP
POTTED BROWN SHRIMP

WINKLES
WINKLES COOKED IN A COURT BOUILLON

MANILA CLAMS
MANILA CLAMS GRILLED WITH BUTTER

RAZOR CLAMS
SAUTÉED RAZOR CLAMS

COMMON COCKLES
COCKLES & CLAMS WITH SEA VEGETABLES

Gathering shellfish

GATHERING SHELLFISH

Sandy mudflats on beaches, foreshores and estuaries are rarely what they seem. They may look like barren uninteresting wastelands but they're a whole universe to thousands of creatures and home to many of our delicious indigenous shellfish. In a word, they deserve *respect*.

When gathering a feed of shellfish, *respect* is as standard and important as your wellies when foraging. *Always* have respect for nature, your surroundings and wildlife and, as with all aspects of hunting and gathering, adhere to these two golden rules: only take enough for a feed and leave nothing but your footprints. *Make your experience memorable for all the right reasons.*

Before setting out prepare thoroughly, a little research prior to any hunting and gathering expedition involving tidal waters is essential. A book of tide tables for the coastal waters you intend to visit is an absolute must and before venturing out on any foreshore or estuary, always check with the *Local Harbour Authority* or *Sea Fisheries District Office* and obtain a copy of any shellfish orders and local bylaws. These will give you all the information you need regarding closed seasons when gathering is and isn't permitted, plus the all-important minimum size limits. Closed seasons may vary from area to area and specie to specie. Taking undersized shellfish is illegal and carries a heavy fine.

Safety: *Always* check fishery orders, area bylaws & tide tables for your designated area.

Standard equipment: wellies, small rake, lightweight 2-gallon bucket, a few 2-litre plastic milk bottles.

ROCK LIMPET Patella Vulgata

Picking season: May to January
Additional equipment: a hand-sized flat stone or sharp knife

The rock limpet or common limpet is a member of the gastropod family, creeping about on a fleshy foot attached to its stomach, as do all slugs or snails. Now, don't let this put you off. When hunting and gathering a foreshore feast the humble rock limpet is a good starting point for shellfish, especially if you're a beginner as it's impossible to get this one wrong.

The suction power of this copious little gastropod is quite amazing and they're rarely dislodged even during violent storms. Actually, limpets thrive in storms as their eggs disperse and become precious plankton. Within two weeks, their larval life is over and the minute limpets settle on the seabed where they quickly attach to the rocks beginning their search for algae, their staple diet.

How to recognise

Rock limpets are impossible to get wrong because of their cone-like shape. They're abundant and vary in size with larger limpets growing to over two inches in diameter. They can be found firmly stuck to rocks and are virtually impossible to dislodge with your bare hands.

Where to find

Rock limpets can only be found in open tidal waters such as seaside rock pools. With their tough flesh and their amazing *stuck like a limpet* suction powers, they can be found in profusion.

Collecting tips

Only gather rock limpets that have been completely submerged when the tide is at its highest, which reminds me, the golden rule when hunting and gathering on any foreshore - be aware and keep a keen eye on the rising tide. It can come in more quickly than you might imagine and the risk of being cut off as the sea level rises can result in serious consequences.

Don't be tempted to think the larger shells will contain the best feed as these are the granddads and will be old, tough and extremely chewy. Select smaller shells no more than an inch in diameter. The only way to dislodge them is with a short, sharp blow with a large stone, or by prising the limpet from the rocks with the point of a sharp knife. I always think of the latter as being the adult method as children with sharp knives scuttling about on slippery rocks really isn't a good idea.

"As shellfish go, limpets aren't my favourite to gather but they really are worth a bash. I love them as a simple starter or in hearty chowder."

How to prepare

Having chosen the smaller, young limpets, make sure they're free of any growth on the shells such as seaweed. Store them in a bucket of cold seawater overnight to allow them to purge themselves and it's always a good idea to remove the dark green, algae-filled gut sack that's hidden in the pointy bit of the shell. After cooking it's easy to find and dispatch.

How to cook/use

The simplest way to cook limpets is to steam them in the shell, after they've been fully rinsed and purged, or sauté them in a bit of butter, garlic and white wine or cider.

For an interesting dinner party starter you'll need a dozen medium-sized limpets per person. I really do recommend you avoid the large ones; they're like chewing a piece of old welly.

To make limpet chowder you'll need two to three dozen cooked limpets. Store them in a tupperware box with the lid on and keep in the fridge.

DEVILLED ROCK LIMPETS
WITH PICKLED SEA PURSLANE
& LEMON TARTAR SAUCE

Serves 4 as a snack
Equipment: deep-fryer

1 kg limpets, cleaned

2 to 3 litres court bouillon (*see page* 191)

500 ml milk

1½ - 3 litres rapeseed oil for deep-frying

crispy laverweed & pickled sea purslane to
    garnish (*see pages* 61 & 79)

Lemon tartar sauce

500 g mayonnaise (*see page* 192)

60 g pickled sea purslane, (if you don't have
    purslane use capers)

60 g gherkins, finely chopped

60 g shallots, peeled & finely chopped

a small bunch of parsley, finely chopped

juice & zest of ½ a lemon

salt & freshly ground black pepper

To prepare the limpets, blanch them in court bouillon for 2
minutes or until just cooked, don't overcook as they'll become
rubbery. Strain and when cool enough to handle, remove from
the shells and cut away the dark stomach bits leaving the
clean light flesh. Cover these with milk and leave to soak until
ready to use.

Preheat oil in a deep-fryer to 180°C. Dredge the milk-soaked
limpets through the devilled flour and deep-fry until golden.
Drain on kitchen roll, season and serve hot on a bed of pickled
sea purslane with tartar sauce.

For the lemon tartar sauce, mix all the ingredients except the
lemon juice together then add enough juice and season to
taste. Chill until ready to use.

*"In the American deep-south devilled oysters are a classic Cajun dish.
They're delicious. This is my British take on it."*

BROWN SHRIMP Crangon Crangon

Picking season: no season but best from April to October
Additional equipment: push-net, small bucket

Brown shrimp play a big part in the estuary food chain – just about everything loves a bit of shrimp for tea and for this reason they do their best to stay out of the limelight. Preferring to feed at night, they spend the day buried just below the sand keeping a watchful lookout with their minute eyes that are mounted on protruding moveable stalks.

How to recognise

Brown shrimp are similar in shape to their cousin the prawn but much smaller. Mature brown shrimp are only three to five cm long but be warned, they're masters of disguise! They are able to camouflage themselves to blend in with the seabed and avoid predators including fish, sea birds and of course the occasional forager with a push net.

Where to find

Brown shrimp can be found just about anywhere around the UK coastline and have acquired numerous colloquial names including: *bay shrimp*, *grey shrimp* and *sand shrimp* – the last of these being its preferred habitat. Unlike their prawn cousins, who prefer to hide within rocky outcrops and dense sea kelp beds, these little fellas thrive in the shallow water of estuaries and harbours on flat, muddy and sandy seabeds.

Collecting tips

A push-net is the essential piece of equipment for catching shrimp and these can either be bought or made at home. The basic construction is a D-shaped hoop with small mesh netting attached to a good long, sturdy handle with a cross bar mounted at the pushing end. The handlebar helps you use your body to effortlessly push the net across the seabed. A small bucket placed inside a large canvas shoulder bag is by far the best collecting method as this will leave both hands free for pushing, manoeuvring and emptying the contents of your push-net.

You can wear anything from chest waders to swimming costumes (no speedos please). No matter, just make sure you wear rubber sandals or a pair of old trainers to protect your feet. Estuaries are also home to weever fish whose sting is pretty fierce. These little devils wriggle into the seabed and lay in wait for their prey. When startled they spread their black, venom-filled dorsal fins just above the sand. A naked foot has no chance and will be left throbbing for hours.

I prefer wading out as the tide is going out, pushing my net in front of me in water just above knee height, lifting the net every ten yards or so to see how I'm doing. I pick out the largest ones and set free the small fry to swim back to safety.

How to prepare

For your return home keep the shrimp alive in a bucket by simply covering them with some freshly picked wet seaweed. Once home, wash off any sandy mud by rinsing them in a colander under a gently running, cold tap. Preparation done – cook your shrimp asap. As with all shellfish, to be humane, pop them in the freezer for about 30 minutes. The cold will put them in stasis so they will go to sleep.

How to cook/use

Bring a pot of well-salted water to a rolling boil and lower in the cleaned shrimp. Stir gently with a slotted wooden spoon and after no more than two minutes strain through a colander and they're ready to eat. The brown shrimp's shell is soft so they can be eaten in their entirety – a tad crunchy but delicious.

Peeling brown shrimp is rather tedious but well worth the effort. Their armour plating is nothing like a prawn's and comes away more easily. Simply pinch off the head and tail using your fingers. With a bit of practice the body shell will come away on the tail end.

"When I think of brown shrimp I instantly want to grab my push-net and head off to the shallow waters of the estuary and content myself with a couple of hours of wading about gathering a good feed of these sweet little beauties."

POTTED BROWN SHRIMP

Serves 4
Equipment: 4 ramekins

210 g brown shrimp, peeled

180 g unsalted butter

juice of one lemon (or to taste)

a generous pinch of ground mace or nutmeg

a pinch of cayenne pepper

1 small bay leaf

1 tsp anchovy paste

salt & freshly ground white pepper

a loaf of fresh sourdough, sliced & toasted

lemon wedges

Melt the butter in a pan, add the lemon juice, mace, cayenne pepper, bay leaf and anchovy paste and simmer on a low heat for 2 minutes to let the spices infuse. Remove from the heat and cool the mixture until it is just warm. Add the shrimp and stir well, then season with salt and pepper. Put the mixture in the fridge and stir every so often.

When the butter starts to set, fill the ramekins. Cover with cling film and return to the fridge until ready to serve but don't serve straight from the fridge as the butter will be too hard to spread nicely on to the toast and won't taste as good. Serve with hot buttered toast and lemon halves.

"This is one of my favourite simple recipes. It's a classic recipe from my J Sheekey days. It's perfect and I still use it in my restaurants today."

WINKLES Littorina Littorea

Picking season: September to April
Additional equipment: large pin or cocktail sticks for shelling

The winkle's one-piece shell makes it easy to identify as part of the gastropod family but getting really over-excited about gathering them is a bit difficult as they don't put up much of a fight to collect and they're quite laborious little fellas to prepare.

How to recognise

Winkle shells are grey to black and easy to spot. They have the same spiral pattern as other snails. They're almost completely round with a slight point at the tail end and quite a large opening from which the invertebrate extends. At low tide winkles seal their bodies inside their shells with the aid of a thin, shiny black or dark brown plastic looking cover that's attached to their foot. It's good to check the occasional winkle when gathering to make sure you can see the plastic looking seal, if it's not there the shell may be empty. During gathering you'll likely collect quite a few deserted shells and you'll soon become expert on recognising live winkles at a glance.

Where to find

Winkles favour a sandy, shingle or stony seabed, especially with small rocky outcrops where they can rasp off fragments of algae with their microscopic, jagged and curved radula teeth. You'll never find winkles running about, as it were; they only feed when the tide is rising and by low tide they'll have found a resting place either stuck to a stone or gathered in large quantities around the base of rocks covered by protective seaweed. Brush the seaweed aside and if you're lucky you'll find a good handful or more. Always remember to replace the overturned weed to conceal the smaller shellfish from predators.

"Across the English Channel, une plateau de fruits de mer isn't complete without a good sprinkling of our winkle friends and the distinct meaty, seaside flavour is well worth the effort. Vive la winkle!"

Collecting tips

These tasty little sea snails can be gathered almost anywhere around the UK coast but, as with most other shellfish, only gather a feed of winkles in the months that have an 'r'. From May through August our little snails of the sea are breeding and should be left alone. When the time is right, only gather the greyish black winkles if they are the same size or larger than marbles. Leave the juvenile winkles to develop and grow.

Large quantities of winkles are essential if you're looking for a good feed. A two gallon bucket full of freshly picked winkles, cooked and removed from their shells with the aid of a pin, will provide you with a small bowlful of edible shellfish.

How to prepare

Tip the winkles into a sink and just cover them with cold tap water. Place an outspread hand on the winkles and roll them around the sink in a clockwise then anti-clockwise motion. This tumbling effect will remove loose debris and clean the shells prior to cooking.

Boil the winkles in salted water for 3 to 4 minutes. Using a pin gently twist the meat from the shell. Once you've got the knack it goes pretty quickly and the delicate flavour is well worth the effort.

How to cook/use

Plain boiled winkles with a splash of vinegar and pepper can be served with bread and butter. Alternatively, remove them from their shells, toss them in hot garlic butter with chopped parsley and a squeeze of lemon. They make an unusual and interesting starter at any dinner party.

WINKLES COOKED IN A COURT BOUILLON
& SERVED WITH MALT VINEGAR

Serves 4 as a snack

1 kg winkles, properly washed

2 to 3 litres court bouillon (*see page* 191)

a splash of olive oil

a few splashes of malt vinegar

sea salt

Before cooking make sure the winkles have been washed in plenty of cold running water then soak them in cold salted water for 30 minutes.

The winkles will need to be cooked for at least 30 minutes or until tender and easily removed from the shell. Once cooked, strain in a colander and roll around with a splash of olive oil. Remove the winkles from their shells with a cocktail stick or winkle pick as we know them and discard the hard foot at the top end. Sprinkle with a bit of malt vinegar and salt. They're a bit fiddly but they're well worth the effort.

"Personally I believe winkles are an acquired taste so anyone who loves eating them has their favourite way to enjoy them. Mine is simply dipped in a little malt vinegar."

MANILA CLAMS Tapes Philippinarum

Although *Manila clam* is the true name of these indigenous molluscs, they are also caught commercially and sold as *palourdes* (*Tapes Decussatus*). The contents of the rounded oval shells are similar in shape and size to a large cockle but they have much meatier flavour and the added bonus that they're less likely to be as gritty as their humble cockle relations.

Manila clams have a limited distribution around British waters but they're spreading rapidly. If you're fortunate enough to live near a harbour or estuary where they can be gathered, always undertake a little careful research by checking with the local *Sea Fisheries District Office* or *Department of Environment* to make certain that raking up a feed of clams is permitted and that you're aware of any fishery orders and bylaws regarding closed seasons and size limits. Once you are satisfied that gathering a feed is legal, getting out and filling your lungs with salty and fresh sea air can only be good for you. Happy hunting!

"Gourmets quite rightly regard these small to medium-sized, superbly flavoured clams as the Grand Cru of the species."

Where to find

Clams are bivalve filter feeding molluscs that live just below the surface of the sandy mud and they thrive where the water is clean. They grow particularly well in brackish water where fresh water streams meet the sea. Never gather shellfish of any kind near outfalls, especially those of the sewage or chemical kind.

How to recognise

Manila Clams and palourdes have heavy, strong shells that are not easily broken or cracked and can vary in colour from cream to grey to pale brown with distinctive black markings. These colourful stripes widen from the back to front, from the hinge of the shell to where the clam opens. The fleshy content of each shell is a creamy oyster brown colour, its foot is similar in colour to the flesh, and this varies from other varieties that have a much brighter, yellowy-orange foot.

Collecting tips

Once you've made certain that gathering a feed of clams is within the law, the next and most important thing to check is the tide table book. A falling or ebb tide is best. Arm yourself with a small garden rake and a couple of sturdy buckets and begin looking for telltale signs such as old shells on the surface of the mud. Another golden rule is never make a beeline for other hunter-gatherers. Believe me, there is nothing more annoying than someone homing in and there is nothing more satisfying than finding your very own little patch of clams and once you've homed in on a couple of small patches a feed will soon be in your bucket.

Raking down just an inch or so at the edge of the water makes gathering much easier. You'll hear that small *plink* sound when your rake makes contact with the shells. As you lift them to the surface, the moving water will wash away the sandy mud from the shells making it easier to recognise at a glance which clams are alive and healthy and helping you sort out the empty shells that abound.

Beware! Occasionally a clam will *look* alive, healthy and tightly closed but, in fact, the two-part shell is just stuck together and filled with black, stinking mud. If unnoticed, these will explode when cooked making your meal inedible. To avoid these ticking time bombs, you *must* wash your clams thoroughly with clean seawater while you're gathering them.

Before leaving the mudflats, cover the clams in your bucket with fresh, clean seawater for your return journey. If you're worried about splashing water all over the inside of your car then simply fill three or four clean, two-litre, plastic milk containers with fresh seawater. Cover the clams on your return home, making sure to leave the clams somewhere cold and dark overnight. This should be sufficient time to flush out any grit and you can then dry the clams and store them in the fridge covered with a damp cloth or kitchen roll where they'll keep for several days prior to cooking.

How to prepare

Place the clams in your kitchen sink or washing up bowl and just cover them with cold tap water. Using an outspread hand vigorously ruck them around in both directions. This will buff up the shells a treat and ensure you haven't missed one of those mud-filled time bombs.

Clams are pretty much grit free but make certain you've given the shells that extra good scrub before cooking. The freshly opened shells with their meaty contents make any dish look fantastic when served.

How to cook/use

As with all shellfish, discard any clams that aren't closed tightly before cooking and any clams that don't open during cooking *must* also be thrown away. Never be tempted to prise them open. Shellfish poisoning can be extremely uncomfortable.

Clams can be used in many ways. Create a delectable dish by cooking them in the same way as mussels using a simple *moules marinières* recipe; steam open in wine with shallots, garlic, parsley and a splash of cream. It's an absolute favourite of mine! Or simply remove the clams from their shells after cooking and toss them in hot garlic butter, then mix with al dente pasta and add a sprinkling of freshly chopped parsley or how about a hearty clam chowder, that gets my thumbs up every time.

MANILA CLAMS
GRILLED WITH BUTTER &
WILD GARLIC BREADCRUMBS

Serves 4

Equipment: food processor, heatproof presentation dishes

1 kg Manila clams, cleaned (a bowlful per person)

6 slices of stale bread

½ bunch of parsley

½ bunch wild garlic

zest of 1 lemon

salt & pepper

100 g butter, melted

a handful of 3-cornered garlic flowers for garnish

slices of fresh warm bread to mop up the sauce.

Place all the ingredients except the clams and butter in a food processor and blitz to a fine breadcrumb.

For the clams preheat oven to grill. Gently steam the clams until opened but not fully cooked then take off the top shell and lay them on a heatproof presentation dish. Sprinkle the clams with the breadcrumbs and drizzle over the melted butter. Bake under the grill or salamander until golden brown. Serve hot with lemon wedges and warm bread.

"At The Savoy we frequently had the French classic, Coquille St Jacques Persillade on the menu. This is my wild version of it."

RAZOR CLAMS Ensis Siliqua

Picking season: May to January, check local area bylaws
Additional equipment: fine salt and eagle eyes

The razor clam is, in my view, one of the best to eat amongst the bivalve molluscs. It's also the most difficult to find. For most, the empty and discarded cut-throat razor-like shells found washed up on the beach are as close as you'll ever get to the real thing but with a little knowledge and know how, locating and catching enough for a good feed can be surprisingly easy.

"Seared razors with chorizo and tomatoes will really get your lips smacking and I'm more than certain will leave you wondering why it's taken so long to discover this strange looking but superior tasting mollusc. Enjoy the whole experience and bon appétit!"

How to recognise

Razor clams are just one of the many bivalve molluscs that typically have a two-part shell hinged by means of a horny ligament and, as with most other bivalves, spend most of their lives living quite deep beneath muddy sand and are known as filter feeders. When the sandy mudflats are covered by the incoming tide, the razors emerge and with shells protruding an inch or so above the seabed they feed by extending their tube-like siphon into the flowing tide. The siphon inhales seawater and the clams extract organic food particles that are captured by a mucus-filtering system in their gills.

Where to find

Razor clams only thrive where the water is impeccably clean. Empty shells washed up on the shore at high tide provide an obvious sign of where to look when the tide is at its lowest. The lowest tides, called 'spring tides', occur shortly after the new and full moon. That's not to say that that you can only collect in the dead of night, spring tides occur twice every month and expose sandbanks that usually stay submerged. At the lowest point of the tide these sandbanks are the best place to start looking for your quarry.

Collecting tips

These delicious little chaps have one tell-tale sign that's extremely difficult to spot; at low tide the razors have a breathing hole concealed with a membrane of saliva mixed with fine silty mud between two minute holes about the size of cocktail sticks and spaced half an inch or so apart. If it rains on the freshly exposed sand at low tide, forget it, you'll never find them and even then, once you've trained your eagle eye and can spot the telltale sign your next problem is how to extract them. Digging is an option but from experience I can tell you it's hard work, not very productive and pretty time-consuming. This combination isn't a good thing when you're racing the tide. Remember, time and tide waits for no man.

The only proven way to gather a good quantity of these mouth watering fellas is to take with you a plastic container full of fine salt. Simply pour half a teaspoon of the salt on the clam's breathing hole. Provided there's a clam beneath, within a couple of seconds it will blow a small amount of water up the hole to dilute a bit more of the salt. Then within a few moments, the clam will rise up from its little

hidey-hole. Now, simply take hold of the shell firmly, but don't snatch or pull at it or you may end up with just the shell. Gently ease the razor clam, complete with contents, out from the sand and into your waiting bucket.

I'm not entirely sure why the salt method works so well. I can only imagine that the clam either assumes that the tide has come back in and is triggered into thinking it's feeding time again, or is simply coming to the surface to try and desalinate from the small overdose of salt.

For commercially harvested razor clams, the length of the shell has to be a minimum size of 10 centimetres or 4 inches. My personal size limit is somewhat larger, more like 12 to 15 centimetres, which is 5 to 6 inches. Personally, I would never embarrass myself by serving anyone a small one!

How to prepare

Razors are the easiest of the filter feeding bivalves to prepare as they are grit, sand and silt free so don't need to be left overnight in a bucketful of sea or salted water. All they need is to be rinsed off in cold, clean water to remove any debris from the shell and simply stored dry in an open container in the fridge.

How to cook/use

If you're going to serve the razor clams as a starter, you'll need 3 or 4 good-sized ones per person and double that for a main course. Cooked simply with olive oil, parsley and lemon juice, or with shallots, garlic and white wine as you would *moules mariniere*, with or without cream, they make a delicious starter or main course.

SAUTÉED RAZOR CLAMS
WITH SPICY CHORIZO, PICKLED ROCK SAMPHIRE, THREE-CORNERED GARLIC & PARSLEY

Serves 4 as a starter or main depending on number of clams (3 for a starter, 6 for a main per person – recipe given as starter so double for a main)
Equipment: bamboo or other stovetop steamer

12 razor clams

a generous splash of white wine

2 shallots, chopped

100 g *A Pinch of Salt* spicy chorizo
 (or equivalent)

50 g rock samphire

3 sprigs wild 3-cornered garlic

a small bunch of parsley, chopped

a splash of rapeseed oil

a knob of butter

For the razor clams, place them in a steamer over boiling water until they just open. Remove the meat from the shells. With a pair of scissors cut out the stomach that can be found about half way down and easily removed, then cut each clam into three and wash the shells for presentation.

To prepare the dish, gently fry the chorizo and shallots in a little rapeseed oil and butter. When golden add the razor clam pieces and cook for a further two minutes. Finally add the rock samphire, three cornered wild garlic and chopped parsley. Scoop the mixture back into the shells for presentation and serve straightaway.

"My butcher, Alan and I make a special range of British charcuterie called, A Pinch of Salt. I cure our chorizo in the traditional Iberian method using spicy paprika and chillies to give it a smoky flavour then I add fennel for a fresh finish. It's perfect for the hearty texture and flavour of razor clams."

COMMON COCKLES Cardium Edule

Picking season: May to January
Additional equipment: enthusiasm

Cockles can be served cold with a splash of white wine vinegar or a squeeze of lemon and seasoned with freshly ground pepper or tossed in hot garlic butter with fresh parsley and lemon. Fried pancetta with cockles tossed in spaghetti is another simple and mouth-watering dish, and using the reserved cooking juices to make cockle and samphire risotto will, I am almost certain, see you time and time again armed with rake and bucket, returning to the mudflats where the cry of herring gulls is always a friendly welcome. Hey, it works for me!

How to recognise

Different to its cousin the clam, cockles are rounded and heart-shaped with heavy ridges running from the back hinge to the front where it opens with distinct coloured rings showing the stages of its growth. They are often gathered on the same seabed as clams and brown shrimp. They can live for up to nine years, though three to four is average.

Where to find

Cockles are widely distributed around the British coastline and can be found quite easily on sandy mudflats at low tide. They spend most of their lives an inch or so below the sediment. At high tide they extend two small siphons above the sediment for breathing and feeding. For moving about the seabed, cockles have a well-developed foot that actually looks more like a tongue. As the tide rises the cockle opens its shell just enough to allow the foot to curl out, then straightening it suddenly, it throws itself freely into the tidal water that washes it along the seabed. It then uses its foot to bury itself into the sand on fresh feeding ground and back to safety from predators.

Collecting tips

Cockles reproduce at an alarming rate. Large cockle beds can contain up to half a million per acre of the sweet tasting delicacies. A mature cockle grows up to two inches. Only collect cockles that measure over one inch across the shell as any under won't have much meat so should be left to grow on.

The simplest and most effective way of gathering a feed is to use a small garden rake. (Using a large rake will only give you backache.) Locating a bed on sandy mudflats is simply trial and error. Start raking in an inch or two of shallow, moving water, as this will wash away the stirred up sand. The raking motion will make it much easier to spot any cockles that lift to the surface.

Half-fill a 2-gallon bucket with clean seawater to wash the cockles as you gather them and change the water often. When you've gathered half to three quarters of a bucketful, add just enough fresh seawater to cover them. Once home, leave them in a cool, dark place as is for 24 hours to give them a chance to flush their systems of sandy grit.

How to prepare

Whilst you're gathering your cockles, thoroughly rinse out two or more 2-litre milk containers and fill them with clean seawater. Seal them tightly for the trip home and refrigerate. To prepare the cockles, rinse them in batches in a colander under cold running tap water. Any cockle that isn't firmly shut should be discarded. Put the cockles in a large, heavy-based stainless steel pot and barely cover them with your bottled seawater. If you didn't collect any seawater, well-salted tap water (25 g sea salt per litre) will do the same job.

"I think cockles are completely underrated, they're naturally plentiful and delicious."

How to cook/use

Bring the pot to a rapid boil, stirring the cockles once or twice with a wooden spoon. After 2 minutes, turn the heat off, put the lid on and allow to cool in their juice for 5 minutes. They are fully cooked when the shells spring open. Any cockle that hasn't opened after cooking should be discarded. Never be tempted to prise open any tightly closed shell, as the cockle within is more than likely dead and definitely not fit for eating.

Carefully strain and pick the cockles from their opened shells while they're still warm and discard the empty shells. You'll find it totally impossible not to try one or two at this stage and you'll be more than a little surprised at just how sweet and succulent this cousin of the clam tastes.

Once prepared, the common cockle has so many varied uses: in soups, cream-rich tarts and pies as well as sauces to serve with fish. They make a great alternative for any clam recipe, especially chowder.

COCKLES & CLAMS
WITH FORAGED SEA VEGETABLES
& CRISPY LAVERWEED

Serves 4 as a light dish
Equipment: deep-fryer

250 g cockles & clams (either or both)

2 tbsp shallots, chopped

1 garlic clove, chopped

100 ml white wine

50 g butter

100 ml double cream

a pinch of parsley, chopped

salt & pepper

6 pieces of crispy laverweed, (*see page* 61)

a handful of samphire, sea beet & purslane,
    washed & blanched

1½ - 3 litres rapeseed oil for deep-frying

crusty bread to serve

In a heavy-bottomed pan heat the butter, garlic and shallot and cook without colour. Add the cockles and clams and white wine and cover with a lid. When they have steamed open add the double cream, season to taste and bring back to the boil for 1 minute then keep warm until ready to serve. Just before serving add the parsley and sea vegetables and leave for 30 seconds to cook in the sauce.

Serve with ample crusty bread and a glass of chilled white wine.

"Cockles are so under-used and a very sustainable food. I wanted to create a dish that showcased the taste of the ocean that I grew up with."

Contents

LAVER
CRISPY LAVERWEED WITH SMOKED SEA SALT

MARSH & ROCK SAMPHIRE
PICKLED ROCK SAMPHIRE

SEA BEET
MUSSELS IN WHITE WINE & GARLIC

SEA KALE
SEA KALE & BROWN SHRIMP

SEA PURSLANE
PICKLED SEA PURSLANE

BLACK-HEADED GULL'S EGGS
SOFT BOILED GULL'S EGGS

gathering seaweed

On the beach

ON THE BEACH

When I was young, family outings were huge picnics 'down the beach' on sunny summer Sundays. Hampers were filled with sandwiches as big as doorstops and great slabs of homemade cake, all washed down with orange squash.

Little did I know that over half a century later I would still be making regular visits to that very same beach. I never tire of the stunning views of the West Solent and the Isle of Wight's rolling hills. Back then low tide rock pools were simply a little boy's playground. Today, they're still my playground but my experienced eyes see a plethora of edible delicacies. My youthful escapades were filled with wonder at the thriving diversity of life that clung to the rocks and lived in the mud and I still feel that same wonder today.

As a child I collected shells and other treasures, whilst squawking black-headed gulls swooped in and greedily eyed our sandwiches. I simply took it for granted that the gulls would be there and the surplus food was intended for them. They were always delighted to entertain us for the price of a few gigantic bread crusts. I look back at those days now as a foreshadow of how my ever-growing hunter-gatherer instincts developed and now especially delight in gathering a clutch of exquisitely delicious gull's eggs.

Today, when out gathering, it's reassuring to know that all seaweeds are edible and that the gathering of gull's eggs is sustainable foraging although it is expressly restricted to licenced and experienced individuals. The more delicate species of seaweeds abound through the summer months and are my favourite but even the 'tough as ol' boots' varieties are full of that wonderful salty seaside flavour that's simply marvellous when added to stocks and stews. The gull's eggs come from nesting colonies, situated out on the estuary marshes sheltered from the sea. Only licenced experts are permitted to gather eggs and even then only during the brief period when gathering promotes colony livelihood.

Safety: *Always* check area bylaws & tide tables for your designated area to be safe.

Standard equipment: wellies, kitchen scissors, lightweight 2-gallon bucket, a larger bucket, large colander, sterilised airtight containers

LAVER Porphyra umbilicalis

Picking season: April to October

Laver, or laverweed, has always been a very Welsh thing, especially in the southwest of Wales where it's part of the daily coastal diet. Once considered poor man's food, this Atlantic seaweed boiled and mashed to a shiny dark green pulp has become more of a delicacy and is now referred to as 'Welsh caviar'. If you're not a caviar fan don't be put off because laver is simply delicious with a flavour like nothing else. As an added bonus, it's extremely good for you as an excellent source of protein, containing iodine, iron and stuffed with vitamins A, B, B2, C and D. For me, this dark green creamy seaside flavour is exquisite.

Before you jump in your car and head off for Wales, stop! You'll be pleased to know that laver is a common seaweed and widely available around the coastal waters of the UK. Only the coldest and harshest winter weather will completely halt its growth.

How to recognise

Laver shows its first signs of life in early March and from April onwards the young fronds spread rapidly. To the trained eye, identification is easy. It grows in large patches and looks like purplish-brown clumps of crinkly cling film. It can take root and grow on the smoothest of rocks or sandy shingle seabed that's exposed by ebbing tides. At low tide on bright sunny days, the fleshy texture of the laver will dry to a crisp and form a skin-tight sheet of weed hugging the rocks or seabed. In this naturally air-dried state it can look dead and inedible when, in fact, all you need do is splash the dried sheets with a little fresh seawater and it'll reconstitute instantly ready for picking.

Where to find

Laver is primarily Atlantic seaweed but can be found growing just about anywhere around the shores of the UK mainly in the intertidal zone between high and low tides. Close to the high tide mark it can be gathered easily when the tidal waters have only just begun to subside. It's pretty versatile stuff though and grows equally well on sandy shingle mudflats when the tide is at its lowest. Laver might look a bit flimsy but it's tough as old boots and can colonise good-sized patches just about anywhere below the high water mark.

"Laver is absolutely and without question my favourite seaweed to eat so when in season I always have plenty of the luscious stuff to hand."

Collecting tips

A good tip is to always try to gather your laver when the weather has been settled and fine for at least a day or two. Fair conditions allow sand and silt stirred up by rough seas to settle. The clear water of calm seas produces the cleanest seaweed as it removes most of the sandy grit and debris that becomes ingrained in the plant's layers. If you pick in rough weather the laver will be gritty, needing care and attention when cleaning. Believe me, just a few small grains of sand are crunchy, unpalatable and will ruin your first time experience, so go for the nice weather!

The rooting system of laver is incredibly strong and able to withstand the full force of stormy seas so the easiest way to gather is by 'plucking' it in the same way you'd pluck a bird for the pot. If you've never been a pleasant pheasant plucker, you simply take hold of a few leafy sheets of the laver and quickly rip them away at an acute angle with a short, sharp jerk tearing it just above the roots. The plant will grow back within a few weeks. If you're fingers aren't strong enough or you find the weed too slippery take a pair of long-bladed kitchen scissors and simply snip off the thin sheets of laver as close to the roots as possible.

How to prepare

After you've gathered half a bucketful of the cleanest laver available, thorough washing is critical. My preferred 'at home' method is on the garden lawn with a large bucket, hosepipe and colander.

Fill the bucket to just overflowing whilst gently plunging and lifting the weed just clear of the water so that any sand and grit will fall free and sink to the bottom of the bucket. Then, taking a small handful at a time, place the washed laver in a colander and rinse again and again, and yet again, until you're certain that every grain of sand, minute shrimp, sand hoppers and other critters have been thoroughly washed away. It's impossible to wash your laver too many times. The same cleaning process can be achieved in a large kitchen sink using the same plunging and rinsing process.

How to cook/use

Squeeze out most of the moisture and place it straight into a large saucepan. I attack it with scissors, cutting vigorously in a random way until my fingers can't take any more. In my experience, this helps to break down the fibres. Next simmer the chopped weed for a good five to six hours keeping the water topped up so the mixture remains quite sloppy for the first four hours. For the final hour or two let the mixture reduce, check it for seasoning, adding a bit of sea salt. As the reduction thickens, purée it with a hand blender then continue reducing until it's the consistency of thick jam and season to taste.

Leave the bubbling gloop to cool, then store in sterilised airtight containers in the fridge. I'm told freshly prepared laver will keep up to ten days but it doesn't last that long in our house. It's rather moreish!

The culinary uses of the freshly prepared laver are endless. Create a simple hearty breakfast by adding a large dollop of it to the frying pan with a couple of dry-cured bacon rashers and serve on hot buttered toast with scrambled eggs. (It sounds basic but it's an absolute 'must try'). Or heat the laver in a hot frying pan with a knob of butter, squeeze in the juice of half a lemon, season to taste and spread on warm baguette croutons and serve immediately as a nutritious nibble. You can add it to anything like lamb stew or use it like spinach in dhal, risotto and ravioli. It even makes a great addition to pesto. Its uses are simply endless!

(Laver can be bought in tins as a product called, 'laverbread'. It has nothing to do with bread at all! It's made by boiling laver in water until broken down, then sautéed in butter or oil with a squeeze of lemon or orange juice and seasoned to taste.)

CRISPY LAVERWEED
WITH SMOKED SEA SALT

Yield: enough for snacks
Equipment: deep-fryer

500 g fresh laverweed (or as much
    as you like)

1½ - 3 litres rapeseed oil for deep-frying

Smoked sea salt

**Equipment: charcoal bbq, wood chips,
foil tin, sterilised kilner jar (see page 15)**

250 g wood chips, soaked in cold water for
    1 hour, then drained

250 g sea salt

Thoroughly wash the fresh laver in cold running water making
sure all grit is removed. If the laver has dried, soaking it in clean
water will reconstitute it almost immediately. Once clean, lay
pieces out on kitchen roll to remove excess moisture.

Preheat deep-fryer to 180°C. Carefully place in pieces of the
laverweed and fry until just crispy. This will only take a few
seconds. Remove with a slotted spoon and drain on clean
kitchen roll.

For the smoked sea salt, set up the bbq for indirect grilling by
putting the hot coals to one side and leaving a cool side to
work from. Toss the wood chips on the coals. Spread the salt
in a thin layer in an aluminium foil pan and place it on the grate
away from the fire. Cover the grill and adjust the vent holes to
maintain temperature at 180°C.

Smoke the salt for 1 hour then cool to room temperature.
When cool store in a sterilised sealable jar.

*"Seasoned salt is a great way to introduce flavour. I have a smokehouse
and experiment with all kinds of infusions to compliment the meats,
poultry and fish that we hot smoke and cold cure. If you don't have one,
it's easy to do on your bbq at home."*

MARSH & ROCK SAMPHIRE

MARSH SAMPHIRE

Salicornia europaea

Picking season: May to September
Additional equipment: rubber bands

As its name suggests, marsh samphire can only be found growing in boggy marshland fed by tidal waters. To me it's simply one of summer's finest delicacies. It's relatively easy to find and so delicious that I start scouting the soft sticky mud for the first shoots in springtime. If the winter has been mild and the spring pleasantly warm a fine feast of small and tender samphire shoots can be on your plate by mid-May.

How to recognise

Marsh samphire is an annual. It germinates, flowers, seeds and dies all within its particular season. The first visible sign of the minute shoots can be seen as early as mid-April, though to the untrained eye the small shoots are not easy to identify. Within a few weeks, the spindly round stems will have grown to an inch or so tall and begun to take on a smooth, almost 'shaved cactus' appearance. Spring sunshine warms the mud and encourages a burst of growth. The prolific little plants sprout side shoots and start to look like a bonsai cactus.

By the middle of August the plants are in full bloom. The tips of each fleshy jointed stem begin to change colour from vivid green to pink and even beetroot red. The flowers are tiny and completely insignificant as they are the same fleshy texture and colour as the rest of the plant and look more like little nodules than flowers. Though edible, they're not at all attractive and should be left to turn to seed and produce next year's crop.

Where to find

Marsh samphire can be found growing in abundance on salty mudflats within tidal estuaries around the coastline of the UK. Its favourite habitat is around the waterlogged fringes of saltgrass marshes and it also thrives along the edges of shallow muddy creeks where the daily surge of incoming tides brings fresh, nutrient-filled seawater that keeps the mud soft and moist and maintains the perfect conditions to create lush green carpets of samphire. The juicy little shoots can also be found growing beyond the high tide mark on marshland ground that gets flooded regularly by high spring tides where the rise in water level occurs every fortnight with each new or full moon.

"Marsh samphire is my favourite of the wild edible samphire plants."

Collecting tips

Marsh samphire grows in such profusion that the easiest way to gather an early May feed is by thinning the seedlings, just as you would a vegetable garden. Picking in this way and by selecting the larger individual plants also gives the carpet of smaller shoots more room, accelerating their growth and with luck, delivering another feed in a week's time which is a good thing.

As the plants develop and the carpet grows, another simple gathering method is to use a pair of sharp scissors snipping the stem of the plant off as close to the sticky mud as possible. Cutting in this way also allows the plant to shoot again and produce seeds later in the season.

As the plants mature they develop a stringy inner core that gets a bit tough. So later in the season it's the less string-like tips that you want. They're well worth a late season feed. Gathering the tips is even easier; simply use your fingers to snap off the succulent ends of the fleshy shoots.

No matter what month, a useful tip when heading off to gather a feed of marsh samphire is to always wear a few rubber bands on your wrist and use these to contain each individual bunch of freshly gathered shoots before carefully placing them in your basket. If you gather the samphire willy-nilly and toss them into your basket loose, you end up with an uncontrollable basketful that'll take forever to sort out when you get back to the kitchen.

On returning home you may find that the smell of the saltgrass marshes has followed you in the same way smoke does from a bonfire. It's a nice reminder of your expedition.

"Pictured above, James' son Rex takes a moment to think about what he wants dad to whip up with his marsh samphire."

How to prepare/use

Place your bunches of samphire in a sink full of cold tap water and wash each individual bunch separately. Carefully separate each bunch by removing the elastic band and rinse them thoroughly, then place in a colander and rinse again this time under cold running water. Be thorough, it's essential that every grain of sand and mud is washed away. Once you're satisfied, replace the elastic bands to keep your bundles manageable prior to cooking. Put the cleaned bunches in a jug or bowl of cold water for about thirty minutes. This will allow them to drink and make them a little less salty after cooking. Store in the salad crisper as you would watercress.

No extra salt is required when cooking marsh samphire as the little plants have absorbed enough from their habitat. The freshly gathered shoots should be steamed or lightly boiled in shallow water for only 3 to 4 minutes depending on how crunchy you like your vegetables. If adding them to a risotto, quiche or salad, they're best blanched then refreshed in ice water as this helps them retain their bright green colour. They should always be added to the dish in the last few minutes of cooking time.

The mature plants develop a backbone that grows from the roots almost to the tips of each fleshy stem. This stringy core is the only part of the plant that isn't edible. It's chewy and as the plant matures becomes even chewier but it comes away easily after cooking. To remove, hold the root-end and scrape away the flesh with a knife or simply suck the bright green flesh from the stringy core in the same way you would a globe artichoke. It's a bit fiddly but well worth the effort.

Samphire shoots and tips can also be eaten raw or pickled adding interesting flavour, crunch and salty freshness to a wild salad. It's perfect with fish but just as delicious with meat. Simply lightly steam the shoots with a good twist of lemon, knob of butter and season with black pepper.

For me, pickled marsh samphire in bubble and squeak on a chilly winter day is a comforting reminder that the short, dark grey days of winter will soon be behind us. Yum!

ROCK SAMPHIRE
Crithmum maritimum

Picking season: May to August
Additional equipment: sharp, curved mushroom knife

Rock samphire, as its name implies, can be found growing in profusion amongst rocky cliffs, outcrops and shingle beaches around the entire coastline of the UK. Most writers give this seashore plant bad press but I say give it a try and experiment with it.... it's free!

How to recognise
Rock samphire is a very pretty, bushy little seashore plant. It looks quite similar to a fat variety of fennel, having similar fern-like fleshy, pointed leaves. The giveaway is to simply crush the leaves and smell the pungent aroma. Rock samphire has an alarming yet interesting flavour when eaten raw, as one of the carrot family, the smell and taste of aromatic carrot eventually comes through. The plants have clusters or umbels of pretty yellow flowers that bloom from the end of June.

Where to find
It can only be found hugging the coastline and grows just above the high tide mark, sprouting from cracks amongst rocks and will also thrive in the poorest soil on bare shingle banks close to the sea.

Collecting tips
A sharp curved mushroom knife is perfect for cutting the stems as close to the rocks or shingle as possible. The leaves can be quite brittle so handle them gently before placing them in your basket in uniform layers.

How to prepare
Wash the stems and leaves carefully under a cold running tap and allow them to drain in a colander.

How to cook/use
The fleshy leaves have an interesting love or hate it flavour. Lightly steamed they can be served as a vegetable. Used very sparingly they can be used raw or when blanched the tender tips of the leaves can be added to salad. For me, rock samphire is best when pickled and is a definite must for your wild pickling list.

PICKLED ROCK SAMPHIRE

Yield: approximately 1 medium jar
Equipment: medium sterilised kilner jar
(see page 15)

100 g freshly picked samphire

1 garlic clove, finely sliced

1 bay leaf

350 ml cider vinegar

1 tsp sugar

6 black peppercorns

1 star anise

2 allspice berries

1 tsp coriander seeds

Clean the samphire thoroughly and rinse under cold water then pat dry with kitchen roll. Pack the samphire into a sterilised jar with the bay leaf and finely sliced garlic.

In a small non-reactive pan (*see page* 199) gently heat the cider vinegar, sugar and spices until the sugar has dissolved and then bring to the boil for 5 minutes. Pour the hot pickling liquid over the samphire straight into the jar. Seal tightly and leave to mature in a cool dark place for 1 month. You can store unopened for up to 6 months but once opened refrigerate and use within a week.

"This is a great condiment and so easy to prepare there's no excuse not to have it readily available. I use it as an alternative to gherkins or capers. Its natural saltiness also makes it a perfect ingredient for salads and makes a great tartar sauce for fish."

SEA BEET Beta vulgaris maritima

It always amazes me that so many of us that live by the coast think nothing of paying handsomely for a tiny bag of 'Popeye's staple diet' – spinach, despite the fact that native sea beet, the granddaddy of spinach is on our doorstep in abundance. All it takes is a pleasant stroll and a lungful of fresh air to gather a good feed.

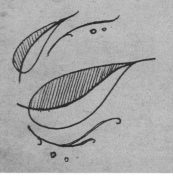

How to recognise

This earthy wild spinach is packed with nutrition and easily identified by its bright green, waxy, veined leaves and can be gathered throughout the year. It grows profusely near the sea and looks just like spinach. Its shiny leaves are somewhat thicker than its cultivated cousins such as spinach, chard or beet.

Sea beet blooms from mid-July onwards when the plants will bolt and send up tall spiky shoots that produce green flowers. These long pointed sprays can be found growing to over one metre in height and look similar to the green millet we use for feeding budgerigars. Young tender leaves can be gathered when the plant is in full bloom then in late summer, after the sea beet plants have dispersed their seeds, the shrivelled woody stems then begin to sprout new shoots. These tight clusters of small tasty leaves grow extremely slowly through the autumn and winter months and are well worth gathering.

Where to find

Sea beet can be found growing in abundance along and just above the high tide mark on saltgrass marshes, overgrown sea defence embankments and even shingle beaches around the UK coast. It's abundant in the south but the further north you go the sparser it becomes.

A south-facing position with protection from cold winds usually produces the best winter pickings. The slow-growing leaves begin to develop as soon as the sun offers spring warmth usually from about mid-March onwards. The larger leaves were once gathered as animal fodder and during the spring sea beet can be gathered 'until the cows come home' but gathering a feed should only take you five minutes or so.

Collecting tips

Sea beet is 'easy pickings' from April onwards. Having made the all-important positive identification select the healthiest looking plants and only pluck a few leaves from individual plants. Please never strip a plant clean of its foliage.

How to prepare

Make certain that you only gather from areas well away from footpaths or anywhere else regularly used by dog walkers. *Need I say more!* As with any plant wild sea beet should be thoroughly washed by soaking and plunging into a sink full of cold water and rinsed in a colander under a cold running tap. Spin off in a salad spinner or pat dry with clean kitchen roll.

How to cook/use

Use sea beet just as you would spinach. Remember that the leaves, being slightly thicker, don't wilt down as quickly as home grown or store bought spinach and holds its shape better when cooked.

The washed and prepared leaves make a delicious addition when used as a layer in lasagne. Sea Beet also makes tasty and extremely healthy soup packed with minerals and vitamins A and C. The larger leaves are great when used as a wrapping leaf like vine leaves. It can be puréed or sautéed with onions and garlic and the plant's firmness makes it an excellent addition to any stir-fry, not forgetting that the fresh young leaves make a delicious addition to any hedgerow salad.

"In my opinion sea beet is far superior in flavour to shop-purchased varieties of spinach and it's free!"

MUSSELS IN WHITE WINE & GARLIC
WITH WILTED SEA BEET

Serves 4

2 kg mussels

2 garlic cloves, finely chopped

800 ml white wine

250 ml crème fraiche

a knob of butter

a large handful or 2 of fresh sea beet, washed

a small bunch of parsley, finely chopped

a handful of 3-cornered garlic flowers to garnish

salt & pepper

To prepare the mussels, rinse them thoroughly in cold water, pulling away the 'beards' and gently scraping away any barnacles. The shells should be shiny and closed tightly. A good hint is that if they are slightly open they should close when you tap them. Discard any that are dry, float, are wide open or do not smell of fresh sea.

Next, sauté half the garlic in butter without colour. Add the rest of the garlic to 1 pint of boiling water mixed with 600 ml white wine then add the mussels. The shells should open fully in only a couple minutes and the flesh should be bright in colour.

Strain the mussels retaining some of the cooking liquor adding a cup of it to the garlic butter. Add some more wine to the mixture then stir in the crème fraiche and let simmer. Season to taste and sprinkle with parsley.

In a separate pan over medium-low heat, drop in the sea beet and gently cook the leaves until just wilted (in the same way you would spinach). Gently squeeze out excess moisture and when ready to serve stir into the finished mussel dish. Serve with a baguette to mop up the sauce.

"These are simply divine."

SEA KALE Crambe maritima

Picking season: April to June

During Victorian times, the humble sea kale was abundant along the shores of the British Isles. It's a bit of a dinosaur of the cabbage family and was widely served as a gastronomic delicacy. It was also frequently used as an elaborate floral decoration and was gathered in large quantities. This had a devastating effect on its population.

Happily, since those bygone days, this spectacular seashore plant has made an amazing and welcome recovery, slowly spreading and re-colonising many areas of the UK coast. Though not endangered, it should be picked sparingly only where there is a plentiful supply and *only then* with permission of the landowner. It would be an awful shame to see this incredibly diverse and lovely plant picked to near extinction once again.

Today, sea kale is grown commercially as the forced shoots of early spring are highly prized by top chefs. The forced plants grow in a similar way to rhubarb and the cuttings and root crowns, or 'thongs', are easily obtainable from horticultural specialists.

In spring, the delicious, asparagus-like flavour of the shoots combined with the colour and shape of the mature plant makes this beauty well worth seeking out. When sea kale is in full flower, the whole plant becomes a mass of delicate and beautifully scented clusters of creamy-white blossoms.

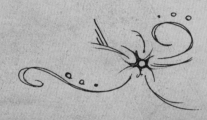

How to recognise

Sea kale is a monster-sized cabbage plant that really does live up to its name protruding from windswept shingle beaches where it would seem impossible for anything to grow. In full bloom, mature plants can reach over two feet in height and radius and are easily spotted from a distance.

Full-grown plants have enormous crinkly, bluish sea-green leaves with a rubbery matt finish. A waterproof waxy coating protects them against the weather-beaten environs they thrive in. As the plants develop, the young stems change colour from dark purple to sea green and eventually the whole plant is covered with large flower-budding heads. The fist-sized flower blossoms release a pungent sweet aroma attracting a great many insects that cross-pollinate the plants.

Young dark purple shoots begin poking their way through the cold shingle in early March. You'll need to get down on your hands and knees, then using your hands like a bulldozer, work your way around the plant and, as carefully as you can, pile the shingle into a mound covering the shoots with twelve inches or more of the shingle to make a stone-like mole hill. Return in two or three weeks and

you'll find curly pink to mauve young leaves just beginning to burst through the pile of shingle. Remove the shingle carefully. If there is no sign of forced growth replace the shingle and come back the following week. Forcing sea kale in this way does no harm and has no ill effect on an individual plant but never force the same plant year-on-year. If you can't find early sea kale shoots in March wait a bit longer, Mother Nature will do her job as winter storms can sometimes bury the plants with several feet of fresh shingle.

Where to find

Sea kale is a salt loving perennial that can only be found growing completely wild by the sea where they positively thrive in the poorest soil conditions. It easily tolerates long spells of drought surviving on moisture absorbed through its deep root system. The crown lies dormant through the coldest winter months and is buried just below the surface and has a pretty spectacular growth rate. As soon as the first spring sunshine begins to warm the shingle, it's full steam ahead and the plant develops at an alarming rate. By the end of June the plants are fully grown exposing marble-shaped pods each containing one seed. A large specimen of this plant is capable of producing thousands of individual globular seedpods. Whilst taking windswept winter walks I

frequently pull off the occasional handful of these 'hard as a bullet' pods and disperse them to assist my little friends and ensure future crops as I continue on my way.

Collecting tips

Clear the shingle mound from around the forced young shoots then using a sharp knife cut just a few of the larger stems as close to their rooting base as possible. The forced stems can be quite fragile so carefully place them in a uniform way in your basket.

If you haven't buried any plants and come across the early spring growth of curly purple leaves by chance, use both hands to carefully part the largest rubbery leaves to reveal the freshest young shoots that are still developing at the base of the plant. Using a sharp knife cut just a few of these from each plant. If you happen to find the plant in its state of giant purple sprouting, only cut one stem per person, as this will be quite sufficient for a good feed. For obvious reasons, please don't plunder an individual plant.

How to prepare

Simply rinse the individual stems under a running tap to ensure you remove sand and grit lodged in the leaves and stems. The smaller forced stems can be steamed whole while any larger stems may need to be cut in half. The young and tender curly leaves that have not been forced, along with the giant purple sprouting heads, also just need to be rinsed under a running cold tap to remove any debris.

How to cook/use

The fragile and delicious stems of forced sea kale, to my taste, are a bit like nautical asparagus and without a doubt are absolutely superb when lightly steamed and eaten just like asparagus. The very youngest leaves of the plant, along with the flower budding heads, are also well worth trying and can be eaten either lightly steamed or used to make a delicious sea kale gratin. They are also a great addition when chopped and added to any bean or vegetable soups and the coarsely chopped stems are excellent when roasting a mixture of vegetables.

"Believe me, wild sea kale purple sprouting is far superior and somewhat larger than any purple sprouting that is home grown or shop bought."

SEA KALE & BROWN SHRIMP
WITH LEMON BUTTER SAUCE
& CRISPY LAVERWEED

Serves 4 as a starter
Equipment: deep-fryer

100 g brown shrimp, peeled

1 bunch of English forced sea kale

a handful of fresh laverweed

a pot of marigold petals

½ a lemon

150 g unsalted English butter

a handful of flat leaf parsley, roughly chopped

1 shallot, finely chopped

1½ - 3 litres rapeseed oil for deep-frying

salt & pepper

Blanch the sea kale in boiling seasoned water until tender and place on plates.

For the crispy laverweed, heat the oil in a deep-fryer to 180°C. Thoroughly wash and dry the laverweed then flash fry it in pieces. You want it to be crispy but keep its bright colour. It won't take long.

For the sauce place the butter in a pan and bring to the boil, watch the butter and when you see a golden brown covering starting to appear on the bottom of the pan add the lemon juice, shallots, parsley and shrimp. Season to taste.

Pour the shrimp and sauce over the kale and decorate with laverweed and the pot marigold petals.

"I love this dish. Spending a day collecting the shrimp, kale and laverweed signals the beginning of the summer for me. We force our own sea kale at THE PIG so our guests can enjoy 'poor man's asparagus' without worrying about affecting or depleting wild coastal stocks. The shrimps and lemon butter make a perfect accompaniment and the crispy laverweed adds a tasty texture to the dish."

SEA PURSLANE
Halimione portulacoides

> **Picking season**: year-round (best in spring & summer)

This succulent, tasty and often overlooked little seashore plant is prolific and widespread around the coastal waters of England and Wales and parts of Ireland. In the south the plant is abundant all year round but further north becomes a bit sparse. Without doubt, the fresh shoots of early spring and summer have the best flavour. Early season shoots always have that special fresh flavour especially when picked and then used before the leaves have a chance to wilt.

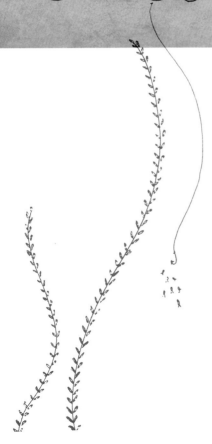

How to recognise

Sea purslane has small oval-shaped silvery grey-green leaves similar to the leaves of an olive tree. It is so abundant and easy to find that if you can't identify this thriving little salty plant of the seashore the life of the hunter-gatherer may be beyond your reach. In other words, it really is impossible to miss and picking a feed is as easy as a Sunday stroll along the shore. Purslane grows at the high tide mark where the highest tides soak and spray the soil.

Where to find

Sea purslane is widespread and grows in large ground covering clumps. This small leaved plant spreads vigorously across saltgrass marshes and can be found growing especially well along the edges of mudflats and creeks throughout entire river estuaries.

Collecting tips

Although fiddly to pick, it doesn't take long to gather a feed by just pinching off the tips of abundant fresh growth. It can be gathered throughout the year but becomes a tad woody through the depths of winter.

How to prepare

Purslane can be prepared in exactly the same way as samphire and it makes a delicious addition to omelettes and quiches when used fresh or lightly blanched. Thoroughly wash the purslane in a sink full of cold water then give it a couple of rinses in a colander under a running tap to ensure that you rid it of mud and grit. If you don't like your purslane too salty, place the prepared shoots in a bowl of fresh water overnight and the succulent shoots will absorb the fresh water and reduce the saltiness.

How to cook/use

Freshly picked purslane tips give a wild salad a subtle hint of crisp saltiness and when lightly blanched or steamed and used as a side dish it takes on a flavour similar to freshly sliced, salty runner beans and great served with most surf & turf dishes. It also makes a great garnish when deep-fried.

"I love the salty crunch of purslane and always keep a pickled jar of it to hand."

PICKLED SEA PURSLANE

Yield: 200 g
Equipment: sterilised kilner jars
(see page 15.)

200 g sea purslane leaves & shoots

400 ml red wine vinegar

¼ cup caster sugar

1 tsp juniper berries, (dried are fine)

1 tsp ground hogweed seed, (optional)

½ tsp fennel seeds

½ tsp cloves

Combine all ingredients in a pan with vinegar and simmer for 10 minutes, then bottle in sterilised jars.

"Like pickled rock samphire, this is a great addition to any salad or condiment for fish and shellfish."

BLACK-HEADED GULL'S EGGS
Larus Ridibundus (black-headed gull)

Picking season: allowed only by regulated license holders from 15 April to 15 May. Available to the public at selected fishmongers and fine restaurants

The black-headed gull is small, long-winged and easy to identify. It has under parts as white as driven snow and the back and upper parts of the wings are pale battleship grey. During the spring breeding months the heads of these elegant birds aren't actually black but rich dark chocolate brown. Through the non-breeding autumn and winter months the colour fades away leaving the head snowy white with a dark spot on each side making the gull look a little like it has four eyes. Their legs, webbed feet and beaks also change colour for the breeding season and turn from a sunburned red to dark crimson. In addition, their shiny black eyes have a fine line of beetroot red around the rim, with a beautiful white eye liner around the back of the eye that looks like it's been painted on by a make-up artist.

The gulls heads begin their transformation as early as February. This is also when the noisy colonies begin building their nesting grounds out on the tidal saltgrass marshes that are cut off by each incoming tide.

Black-headed gulls venture considerable distances inland and will gladly scavenge food from landfill sights. Large flocks of these extremely vocal gulls can also often be seen fighting for pole position whilst following the freshly overturned soil of a farmer's plough.

Squawking en masse and sounding vaguely similar to a pack of hyenas, black-headed gulls have also discovered that invading unsuspecting day trippers at harbours and quaysides, is yet another way to quench their greedy appetites. Every gull tries to out-squawk his nearest rival in an ever-increasing advance to make fish & chip-munching tourists give up their picnics. As one of the smaller variety of gulls they're no match for their aggressive cousin the herring gull so the little chaps usually only manage to win a free meal when they're the first to the picnic.

How to recognise

The gulls Latin name *ridibundus* means 'laughing' and particularly at the onset of the mating season it's easy to see how they acquired their name. The male and female birds perform a noisy squawking display with heads held high, wings folded, but slightly drooped and tail feathers spread wide as the happy couple paddle around each other squealing and cackling at the top of their voices. The noise intensifies as they pair up. The colonies grow and they begin to stake their claims in preparation for nest building on the highest area of any saltgrass marshes that stretch out into estuaries dotted around the UK and particularly the waters of the Solent, between the mainland and the Isle of Wight, close to where I live.

As their winter plumage begins its annual transformation, the ever-increasing number of gulls begins to make considerable noise late into the night. It's a time of excitement on the high ground of our saltgrass marshes as they squabble over partners, nesting sites and even steal each other's building materials. In fact, the density of the nests can become so great that it's almost impossible to step between them during the short egg-collecting season.

For such a cacophonous bunch, their eggs are delicate, exquisite and no two look the same. Each bird tries to mimic its surroundings. The golf ball sized egg-shells are pale to dark olive green, with varying sized flecks of black, brown and grey, making each egg unique and extremely well camouflaged in an attempt to hide the freshly laid eggs from predators such as great black-backed gulls, the occasional heron and of course the sly old fox.

Where to find

Nest building begins in earnest in early April and by the middle of the month a few of the most mature gulls are beginning to lay eggs. Unfortunately for these birds, this is a complete waste of time and effort as, with the new or full moon, high spring equinox tides flood the saltgrass marshes. The catastrophe worsens if the spring tides coincide with heavy gales. Havoc is wreaked amongst the colonies causing nests and eggs to be washed away but as soon as the highest tides subside our tenacious little friends simply get stuck back in and start over again with even more squabbling over the high ground.

"Black-headed gull's eggs are Mother Nature's idea of pure luxury."

Collecting tips

Collecting gull's eggs is only permitted with a strictly regulated licence issued to just a handful of real locals. The licences have been handed down for generations. Each holder is permitted to gather only a stipulated number of eggs and must record on a daily log sheet the numbers collected and the particular area of the marshes from which they were gathered.

The season opens on April 15th though very few eggs are found until the end of the month. The final day for collecting is May 15th. During this short and hectic season, the licence holders, or *Eggers* as they're affectionately known locally, have to be off the saltgrass marshes by 9:00 a.m. from Monday to Friday and 11:00 a.m. at the weekends. These weather-beaten men know the saltgrass marshes like the backs of their hands and detailed knowledge of the terrain is essential as it's a maze of water-filled creeks and dangerously soft, muddy crevices. Venturing onto the marshes has to be treated with the same caution as finding your way through a minefield; in some areas you could find yourself waist deep in sloppy, black, stinking mud if you're not careful!

Eggers begin as early as 5:00 am working swiftly and efficiently to make certain the lively colonies aren't disturbed for too long. This controlled industry is, in my view, absolutely no different to collecting fresh eggs from your hen-house chickens. The gulls, like poultry birds, will continue to lay beautifully camouflaged eggs each and every day while the eggs are taken through the short egging season. Fortunately for the gulls, the licensed egg collecting comes to a halt on May 15th and the noisy gulls then fill each nest with three or four eggs in as many days and begin the incubation period which takes between 20 to 26 days. The saltgrass marshes then become an enormous crèche with quite literally thousands of mottled, light brown, very hungry chicks. This really is the time to guard your picnic!

The controlled tradition of collecting eggs has shown no adverse effects on the numbers of black-headed gulls. The current population is stable at about twenty thousand pairs nesting within the estuaries located throughout the Solent and their success continues even though the gulls face constant threats from all that Mother Nature can throw at them.

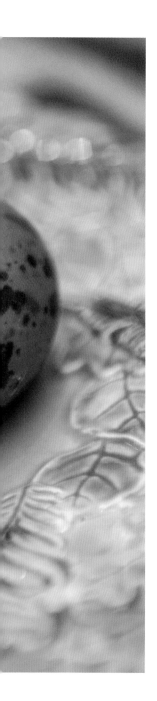

The most noticeable of these threats is the natural erosion of the saltgrass marshes that has seen the gulls nesting grounds diminish at an alarming rate forcing them to nest closer to the shoreline. These areas, despite being cut off from dry land by every incoming high tide, are more easily accessible to raiding foxes, not only gorging on the bountiful glut of fresh eggs but also killing countless numbers of chicks. Even with their amazing camouflage the fledglings have no chance against a cunning vixen with little ones of her own to feed.

The black-headed gull chicks grow at an incredible rate and their fluffy warm down soon turns to feathers and the young gulls take to the wing within 40 days of hatching. By February in the following year, the chicks that survive their first winter begin to develop their first chocolate brown heads and pair up in their squawking colonies for yet another breeding season.

How to cook/use

In bygone years, fresh gull's eggs were a staple part of coastal diets served by the half dozen boiled, scrambled or fried. They were also used to barter with anyone from your local butcher to alehouse landlord. Nowadays, most of the eggs are boxed up in flat trays and on their way to London well before breakfast. You'll find them in top restaurants served gently boiled with green salad, mayonnaise and celery salt. So if you've never tasted this exquisite springtime delicacy put it on your bucket list. They really are that good!

Black-headed gull's eggs are very fragile so be careful when wiping away any mud, debris or guano. A clean damp cloth works well. Bring a large pan of water up to a simmering slow boil, the shells of the gull's eggs being extremely thin can easily crack so, using a large slotted or perforated spoon very carefully lower the eggs into the pan of simmering water. After a maximum of seven minutes, remove the eggs and refresh in ice-cold water. With the shells removed the albumen or white of the egg is in fact semi-transparent with a beautiful hint of blue and the yolk, which should be cooked through with the very centre being almost gooey, but not runny, is a startling flame orange in colour. Bon appetite!

SOFT-BOILED GULL'S EGGS
WITH CELERY SALT & PICKLED SAMPHIRE SALAD

Serves 2 for brunch

6 black-headed gull's eggs

a bowl of iced water

a basket of your favourite wild salad ingredients

a jar of pickled samphire (*see page* 67)

Dijon salad dressing

celery salt

Dressing

1 tbsp grainy Dijon mustard

1 tsp coarsely cracked black pepper

2 large shallots, finely chopped

80 ml red wine vinegar

250 ml olive oil

a pinch of sugar, if needed

salt & pepper

Bring a pan of water to the boil and when ready carefully lower in the eggs and boil for 3 minutes. Remove with a slotted spoon and plunge into iced water to stop the cooking process.

For the dressing, combine all ingredients and season to taste. If the vinegar is too strong add a little sugar to balance the flavour.

Garry's favourite celery salt

I only use the leaves of the celery because the flavour and colour is more intense, so choose celery stalks that are as leafy and rich in colour as possible.

Cut and wash the leaves of several whole stalks of celery (approximately 2 to 3 cups full). Lay them completely flat on cling film so that they form a single layer, not bunched and blast on high in a microwave for 10 seconds at a time. Check between each 10 second interval until the leaves are dry and crispy. Add them to a generous amount of good quality rock salt in a mortar and crush to your desired consistency with a pestle. Garry likes it a bit chunky.

*"Black-headed gull's eggs are so luxurious.
The season is short but they are worth seeking out.
They're quite rich so the pickled samphire salad lifts them perfectly."*

horn of plenty

Contents

CEP & SUMMER CEP
WILD CEP WITH SCONES'

OYSTER MUSHROOMS
OYSTER MUSHROOMS WITH
 BARTLETTS BLACK PUDDING
 & DUCK EGG
STINGING NETTLE PAPPARDELLE WITH
 SAUTÉED WILD MUSHROOMS

HORN OF PLENTY
HORN OF PLENTY, SMOKED SALMON &
SCRAMBLED EGGS ON TOAST

CHANTERELLE & FLOWER OF THE WOOD
A PINCH OF SALT COPPA SALAD

HEDGEHOG MUSHROOMS
HEDGEHOGS & OYSTERS ON SOURDOUGH

CRAB APPLES
NEW FOREST WOOD PIGEON
 & CRAB APPLE FRITTERS

SWEET CHESTNUT
CHESTNUT ICE CREAM

The forest floor & more

ON THE FOREST FLOOR

THE PIG in the Forest and Lime Wood hotels offer their guests three hour guided foraging excursions where I take them out on a variety of walks through the New Forest, on the foreshore of the West Solent and along local hedgerows. The greatest interest remains a walk through the forest. It's no wonder, the ancient woodland that surrounds both hotels is just about the finest and most rewarding place to gather mushrooms but for me there is so much more. Throughout the year the forest is filled with a wonderful variety of berries, nuts, fungi, fruit and edible plants. Guests are always amazed and intrigued by the colours, textures and varieties that spring to life before their eyes.

When conditions are perfect, many different varieties of wild mushrooms can be found growing in abundance throughout the year but autumn is by far the best season to find a tasty feed with the added bonus of being able to reap a harvest of other fruits and nuts. Two of my favourites are wild chestnuts and crab apples and they always end up in my basket so I've snuck them in here too.

Safety: even the smallest amount of the wrong mushroom can be lethal. Knowledge of how to identify edible mushrooms is essential as well as a good guidebook and expert second opinion. Always check area bylaws for your designated area.

Standard equipment: sharp knife, basket or trug.

There are more than two thousand varieties of fungi and mushrooms growing in the UK many of which are edible but my picking list is limited to about twenty. This book is all about my seasonal favourites so, with this in mind, I've selected a few that I think are the finest for eating.

Mushroom picking season in the UK is usually from September until the first frost but mild winters over the past decades have made it possible to gather edible fungi almost throughout the year; only prolonged periods of extreme cold and frost or particularly wet weather will halt their growth.

Before setting out you *must* obtain the permission of the landowner. If you intend to gather from anywhere like the New Forest, which is managed by the *Forestry Commission*, check with them regarding any bylaws and/or recommendations they have in place. Once you've obtained the necessary permission, all you need is a sharp knife (preferably with a locking blade for safety) and a wicker basket with a carrying capacity of four to five kilos. The basket will allow spores to drop as you carry on walking through the forest.

The safest way to pick mushrooms is with a professional guide. Purchase a good photographic reference book and start by taking pictures of specimens that are in perfect condition. There are wild mushrooms out there that can kill you – ingesting even the smallest amount the deadly toxins attack your liver and kidneys. There is no known cure. The number of *poisonous* fungi growing in any particular forest or wooded area can, during some mushroom seasons, be found in prolific quantities growing alongside edible varieties. It takes years to gain enough knowledge to distinguish between poisonous and edible varieties and the ability to identify them at every stage of their growth. I've personally seen young and small deadly poisonous mushrooms picked and placed in a basket, having been confused for deliciously edible cep – the result could have been tragic!

Finally, mushrooms play a very important role in the fragile ecosystem of any forest floor and unless you're gathering for a feed they should be admired, photographed and left to grow. The fear of poisonous mushrooms can have a strange effect on some people. There is nothing more annoying to me than finding beautiful mushroom patches that have been kicked over or beaten apart with sticks.

CEP (ALSO CALLED PENNY BUN & PORCINI) & SUMMER CEP
Boletus edulis & Boletus aereus

Picking season: August to November (*boletus edulis*);
July to September/October (*Boletus aereus*)

Cep, penny bun or porcini, call this mushroom what you like but in my mind this particular variety of fungus really is the king of all mushrooms. It's been highly prized for its superior flavour and texture by a great many chefs for a very long time. Across the English Channel, our European neighbours relish the family tradition of mushroom hunting, venturing into the woods at weekends armed with baskets, sticks and penknives and, more often than not, a pretty impressive picnic basket as well.

"This is the king of all mushrooms"

How to recognise

This big, fat beauty of a mushroom has a thick, scaly-looking, ivory-coloured stem topped by a smoothly rounded, chestnut-brown cap. On the underside are the gills that are in fact, minute tubes that resemble a sponge-like profusion of microscopic holes. These gills are pale cream when the cep is young and change colour to olive green as the mushroom grows. Although some people still collect the olive-coloured mature mushrooms for drying, it's my view that beyond this stage the cep is past its sell by date and best left to nourish the forest floor.

Where to find

The preferred habitat of our chunky friends is the ground beneath mature oak trees. They always grow particularly well around the edges of forest glades where the grass has been grazed hard by animals. They are unlikely to grow in any quantity in broad daylight beyond the tree line on open ground, as they prefer the light, but not direct heat, of the sunshine whilst sheltered beneath the canopy of the oaks.

On rare occasions I've seen ceps growing in areas the size of three or four football pitches where you could pick so many that it'd be impossible to carry them out in one go. It doesn't happen often but it's amazing when it does. Over the years, experience has taught me that picking wild mushrooms in reasonable quantities has no ill effect on the ecosystem of the forest. The spores for next year's crop begin to disperse soon after the caps begin to unfold and the gills are revealed. Mushroom patches need to be treated with respect. Individual rows and patches of the different varieties I pick return year-after-year when the conditions are right.

Collecting tips

When out gathering wild mushrooms, always try to be as quiet as possible so not to disturb any of the abundant wild life. You won't see any if you're too noisy. Think of yourself as a guest in their home. When you've located and positively identified your mushrooms hold the stem carefully and gently twist the individual fungi from its roots. Any hole left in the forest floor should be filled to protect the mycelium. Then brush or cut away any dirt or leaf litter before carefully placing each mushroom in your basket. Mushrooms will bruise and can easily break apart. A basketful of battered, broken mushroom pieces isn't very useful in the kitchen.

How to prepare

Never wash wild mushrooms under a running tap as they're porous and become waterlogged and useless for cooking. Brush them with a clean, dry pastry brush, or wipe the caps and stems with a clean damp cloth. Store your prepared wild mushrooms in small opened top containers in the fridge. Freshly picked mushrooms will keep for two weeks or more if you turn them occasionally. That is, if you don't scoff the lot!

How to cook/use

Ceps are one of the wild mushrooms that can be eaten raw unlike many wild varieties that have to be thoroughly cooked to remove poisonous toxins. For this reason alone, I would not advise anybody to eat wild mushrooms raw. For beginners the safest way is to sauté freshly picked cep in a little olive oil and a knob of butter in a hot frying pan until they just begin to turn golden brown, then pop them onto fresh toasted bread and drizzle with the juices.

Their exquisite flavour lends ceps to countless culinary uses but no matter how you cook them they're always delicious. Use them any way you like: pan-fried, sautéed, in soups, pies, risotto or stews. I can guarantee that once you've delved into the world of these magically tasting mushrooms, a punnet of clinically grown, farmed chappies just won't have the same appeal.

SUMMER CEP *Boletus aereus*

There is one member of the *Boletus* family that can be gathered during July and September but only when these two months are horribly and unseasonably wet. The *boletus aereus*, alias the summer cep, is as delicious as the *boletus edulis* but slightly different in colour and can be cooked and used in exactly the same way as the cep. The cap of the summer cep is dark matt brown, similar in colour to many of last year's fallen leaves and, being quite short and stumpy with a teak brown stem, is camouflaged to perfection and extremely difficult to spot when growing amongst the leaf litter beneath the oaks.

WILD CEP
WITH MUSHROOM & POTATO SCONES

Serves 2

100 g potatoes, cooked

100 g self-raising flour

25 g butter

75 g Lyburn *Winchester* cheese

a handful of mixed garden herbs, chopped
(thyme, parsley or rosemary)

1 tbsp olive oil

450 g mushrooms, chopped, (beefsteak,
portobello or flatcup)

225 g wild cep, sliced

6 shallots, peeled & finely chopped

1 garlic clove, puréed

a small bunch of fresh thyme, chopped

a large knob of unsalted butter

fresh black pepper and sea salt

For the scones, mash the potato with a little seasoning. In a separate bowl, sieve the flour and rub in the butter with your fingers to a crumbly consistency then mix into the mash along with the cheese and herbs. Next heat the olive oil in a skillet and fry the chopped mushrooms (not the wild cep) and add to the potato mix. Pat the mixture into 5cm rounds to form scones. Heat a pan with oil and butter and add the individual scones. Cook until golden brown on both sides.

For the wild cep, clean the mushrooms well, peel and slice thinly. Sweat the shallots, thyme and garlic in a large knob of butter until soft then add the mushrooms, season well and cover with water. Cook until the liquid forms a thick sauce and serve warm with the scones.

(If wild cep are out of season, use dried by reconstituting them in warm water.)

"Lyburn Farm is local to us in the New Forest and makes some of the finest cheeses anywhere. Their classic Winchester is a yellow cheese, made in the style of Gouda but aged like mature Cheddar. The result is splendid – it's creamy, nutty and sharp at the same time so perfectly balances the wild cep that can be picked in the forest behind the pastures where they graze their cattle."

OYSTER MUSHROOMS

Pleurotus cornucopiae & Pleurotus ostreatus

Picking season: March to December

Don't be put off by the name of this variety of mushroom as they really don't taste a thing like our round, flat, native oysters. They take their name from their shape and look just like fleshy oysters sprouting from a fallen tree trunk. There are two main varieties: *pleurotus cornucopiae*, which is pale, magnolia cream in colour and the more common variety and *pleurotus ostreatus*, that can vary in colour from pale purple to handsome charcoal grey.

How to recognise

As oyster mushrooms begin to grow they develop perfectly curved rims. As they mature the edges become wavy and lobed and can begin to split, though always retaining that slightly downward curve that acts as an umbrella to protect the large white gills beneath.

Oyster mushrooms can be found growing in layers from the decaying bark of fallen beech trees. A word of caution, the largest mushrooms, being the oldest, are frequently maggot ridden so I tend to leave them alone. Sprouting from beneath the larger mushrooms and decreasing in size are the young fresh ones. Some grow with individual stems while others grow in clusters from a single stem.

Oysters are fast growing. The older mushrooms take on a yellow tinge and are past their sell by date so should be left. Their growing season is one of the longest among the wild varieties in the mushroom kingdom and they can be gathered from as early as March.

Where to find

The best place to begin hunting for oyster mushrooms is an area where fallen beech trees have been blown down during the previous year's storms. They can be found sprouting in profusion from the bark of the trunk or even the large limbs. They're at their best from mid-to-late April onwards especially if there's been a week or so of settled weather with good amounts of sunshine and a little rain. A two hour walk in a lovely beech wood can usually yield a basketful or more, plenty for a good feed with any surplus perfect for home drying.

It takes roughly twelve months from the time a beech tree falls for an oyster's windblown spores to settle allowing the mycelium to grow beneath the bark and begin digesting the tree. What we call decay, the mushroom calls breakfast, lunch and dinner!

When conditions are right, with the correct amount of moisture and optimum temperatures, the fruit bodies explode out through the bark, sometimes in eyebrow raising quantities. During the height of the summer, through June, July and August the mushrooms are still available though a particularly warm and prolonged dry spell will see them either shrivel to nothing or be eaten by maggots.

Collecting tips

When a fallen beech tree first begins to fruit with oyster mushrooms, the young fresh fruiting bodies are almost rubbery to the touch. Always check the underside and only gather the mushrooms with snow-white gills. Any discolouring will give away their age. You can also easily check for maggots by cutting off one mushroom then simply tearing the oyster through the gills from front to back. This will reveal any unwanted inhabitants.

Gather mushrooms that are larger than a hen's egg and leave the smaller ones to grow on. Using a sharp knife, carefully slice the mushrooms off as close to the bark of the tree as possible. Gathering a feed in this way doesn't interfere with the mycelium, giving the oysters the ability to sprout more fruiting bodies to gather the following week.

How to prepare

Avoid gathering oyster mushrooms just after heavy rain, as like many mushrooms, they are very absorbent. Never wash them for the same reason. Oysters are not as delicate as many other varieties. You can simply wipe the tops clean and brush away any debris from the gills. Excess moisture can be removed by sandwiching them between layers of kitchen roll then gently squashing the moisture out. Trying to pan-fry wet mushrooms will only result in stewing them. Yuk.

How to cook/use

As with all wild mushrooms, I would not advise anybody to eat them raw. For beginners the safest way is to sauté freshly picked oysters in exactly the same way as you would ceps or other varieties. Simply sauté them in a little olive oil and a knob of butter in a hot frying pan until they just begin to turn golden brown, then pop them onto fresh toasted bread and drizzle with the juices.

"Over the years I've seen fallen giant beeches covered with so many of these little fellas that you'd have needed a pick-up truck to carry them all out of the forest but a basketful is always quite adequate for me."

OYSTER MUSHROOMS
WITH BARTLETT'S BLACK PUDDING & DUCK EGG

Serves 4

250 g wild oyster mushrooms, cleaned &
   thickly sliced

4 duck eggs

8 1.5 cm slices of *Bartlett's* black pudding
   (or equivalent)

a small bunch of wild sorrel, chiffonade
   (parsley will do)

a knob of butter

salt & freshly cracked black pepper

slices of toasted sourdough to serve

Heat the butter in a skillet and gently sauté the mushrooms until just softening. Over medium heat, crack in the duck egg, lay the pudding slices into the white and sprinkle with the chopped herbs. Season with a bit of salt and pepper and cook until the white is cooked and the yolk still runny. Serve with fresh toast.

*"This is a simple dish and makes me think of being out in the woods.
It's a fry-up but sometimes rustic and basic just can't be beat.
My butcher, Alan Bartlett makes a stunning black pudding
that adds so much richness and flavour."*

STINGING NETTLE PAPPARDELLE
WITH SAUTÉED WILD MUSHROOMS

Serves 4 to 6
Equipment: food processor or hand blender, plastic squeeze bottle, rolling pin or pasta press & drying rack (optional)

600 g stinging nettle pappardelle
(approximately 120 to 150 g per person)

a punnet of wild mushrooms, cleaned & sliced, (10 to 15 g dried mushrooms)

100 g unsalted butter

a splash of olive oil

1 garlic clove, finely chopped

a splash of white wine

a dollop of double cream

a handful of sea beet, cleaned & wilted

a small bunch of flat-leaf parsley, chopped

salt & pepper

Lyburn *Old Winchester*, (or Parmesan)

Stinging nettle pasta

200 g strong flour (tipo '00')

7 egg yolks

50 ml stinging nettle purée

a splash of rapeseed oil

ice

Nettle purée

140 g young nettle tips, washed & chopped

a few ice cubes

2 tbsp water

salt & freshly ground black pepper

If using dried mushrooms, reconstitute them by soaking in boiled water for 10 minutes.

To make the stinging nettle purée, bring a saucepan of salted water to a rolling boil, add the nettle tips, cover and return to the boil. Drain the nettles and refresh under cold water. Blend the drained nettles in a food processor with 3 to 4 ice cubes and just enough water to make a smooth purée. Season to taste.

For the pappardelle, blend the flour, egg yolks and stinging nettle purée in a food processor until a dough is formed. Leave to rest in a refrigerator for 1 hour before use. Roll through a pasta machine to a fine thickness - 1 on machine then cut into thick pappardelle strips. Blanch for 20 seconds in boiling, salted and oiled water and refresh in ice water. You can then cook them in boiling water as you need them or warm them and serve al dente.

To prepare the mushrooms and sauce, melt half the butter in a large pan over medium heat. Add the garlic and cook without colour. Add in the mushrooms and sauté until soft then splash in a bit of white wine. Let the moisture reduce to a saucy thickness then stir in a dollop of whipping cream and a sprinkle of *Old Winchester*. When the cheese is fully melted, add a handful of parsley and melt in the remaining butter to give the sauce a lovely shine. Finally stir in the wilted sea beet. If the sauce thickens add a bit of the mushroom liquor. Season to taste and keep warm.

When ready to serve, toss the al dente pasta into the mushrooms and sauce. Serve in deep pasta plates and top with some extra *Old Winchester*, slices of bread to mop up the sauce and a crisp Italian white wine.

"This is a wild take on an Italian classic. When we photographed this dish oyster mushrooms were the only ones in season but the dish works equally well with cep or others. Yum."

HORN OF PLENTY

(ALSO CALLED BLACK CHANTERELLES & TROMPETTE DE LA MORT)
Craterellus cornucopioides

Picking season: mid-September to mid-November

Don't let this little treasure's ominous name put you off. I can assure you that out of my list of top ten edible fungi it comes in near the top. It is quite simply delicious. Whenever I take friends out to hunt and gather wild mushrooms and we come across an area of trompette, I always ask them to decide whether or not this particular variety of fungus looks edible or poisonous and it always gets the poisonous vote. I then ask them if they would like to sit and rest for a few moments while I gather a feed, which is usually greeted with gasps of 'you are joking aren't you?'

How to recognise

If its French name isn't enough to make you give this mushroom a wide berth the look of it might certainly put you off. It has matt grey to black outer walls rising up to a blackish, dirty brown trumpet opening at the top. The English, 'horn of plenty' refers to the horn or funnel shape. Though extremely well camouflaged with their curled, wavy edges and very irregular shapes you'll very rarely find solitary mushrooms. Once you've located your first mushroom and 'get your eye in' you'll have a basketful large enough for a fresh feed and enough left over for home drying in no time. Finding the first one is the trick!

Where to find

Although this is one of the most difficult wild mushrooms to find, it's worth the effort. It takes a fair old rummage through their preferred habitat amongst the leafy litter of a deciduous beech wood. If you're fortunate enough to locate a patch, gathering a feed doesn't take long. Our rather strange looking fungi friend really does live up to its name and in a good year this master of disguise can be found growing almost like a carpet, covering quite large areas.

Decaying leaf litter acts as insulation for the horn of plenty and protects the mushrooms from frost. As long as the weather remains dry the black trumpets can grow up to eight inches tall making them the perfect size for home drying. They're a lightweight of the mushroom family and shrink to less than half their original size when dried, but they dry very well.

"The French name for the horn of plenty is trompette de la mort or 'trumpet of death'. With a name like that who in their right mind would even pick them, let alone eat them?"

Collecting tips

When picking horn of plenty, take hold of the hollow stem as close to the forest floor as possible then simply twist the mushroom from the ground, nip the dirty root-end off between your thumb and finger and give the mushroom a gentle shake while holding it upside down. This will help dislodge any bugs such as spiders, woodlice and slugs that have crawled inside; even the fruit fallen from the surrounding trees, such as beech mast, can become lodged inside these funnel shaped, almost trap-like fungus.

How to prepare

To make absolutely certain that you're not cooking slugs and bugs with your mushrooms, rod each hollow mushroom through using a small soft artist's paint brush or to make sure you dislodge any unwelcome guests, shake and gently tap each mushroom against the side of your basket or simply split each mushroom in half.

How to cook/use

As with all wild mushrooms, I would not advise anybody to eat them raw. For beginners the safest way is to sauté freshly picked horn of plenty in exactly the same way as you would ceps or other varieties. Simply sauté them in a little olive oil and a knob of butter in a hot frying pan until they just begin to wilt, then pop them onto fresh toasted bread and drizzle with the juices.

HORN OF PLENTY, SMOKED SALMON & SCRAMBLED EGGS ON TOAST

Serves 4 for brunch

250 g horn of plenty (black trompette), sliced

4 generous slices *A Pinch of Salt* smoked salmon, (or equivalent air-cured)

4 large free-range eggs

100 ml milk

slices of sourdough, toasted

a few generous knobs of butter

salt & freshly cracked black pepper

In a warm skillet sauté the mushrooms in a knob of butter until just soft and keep warm. Whisk together the eggs and milk and lightly season. Warm a clean skillet with a bit more butter and cook the egg mixture over medium heat until fully cooked but still soft.

Toast and butter the bread and place a slice of salmon on each then top with the eggs and mushrooms. Season to taste and serve hot. Voila!

(As with all wild mushrooms horn of plenty are seasonal. If they aren't available, reconstituted dried or a different variety will work equally well.)

"This is another simple dish. Luscious ingredients don't need to be complicated to be great."

WINTER CHANTERELLE

CHANTERELLE (ALSO CALLED GREY CHANTERELLE & YELLOW LEGS)

Cantharellus infundibuliformis

Picking season: September to December

For most mushrooms, the first frosts of winter signal the end of their growing life; not so for this hardy little chap. I've seen the winter chanterelle completely frozen solid and amazingly when thawed, it has continued to grow. The thing that will finish them off however is too much rain followed by prolonged and harsh ground frost. With a completely hollow stem and a funnel shaped cap, the little mushroom will finally give up and rot back into the ground. Still, it's done its job of decomposing and digesting the fallen rotting remains of trees, mainly pine, and dispersed countless thousands of spores into the forest air so it's a dignified end. This insignificant looking mushroom can be found in good quantities almost every season so, as long as the conditions are right, the army of winter chanterelles will be back next year.

How to recognise

All three common names are quite appropriate. 'Yellow legs' is a great description as the stem of this quite small mushroom can be almost as bright as a buttercup. The name 'grey chanterelle' refers to the colour of the funnel-shaped cap with its irregular wavy edges that are actually pale yellowy-brown when the mushroom first appears from beneath the forest floor. As the fungus grows the gills beneath the frilly golden-brown cap begin to release their spores and coat the underside with grey dust that gives its name.

Where to find

The name 'winter chanterelle' should give you a clue as to when this mushroom grows. Its preferred habitat is amongst mature coniferous trees where the mushroom thrives on the acid soil, especially where the pine trees have been 'brashed' which is simply the cutting of the lower branches to allow the tree to grow tall and straight. These branches are left on the forest floor and as they wither our little winter chanterelles get to work decomposing and digesting every last morsel.

"Serve this little mushroom fresh. The delicate, delicious flavour is really yum. Pan-fried, on toast, in risottos, stews or pies, take your pick, they're just delicious."

Collecting tips

Being quite small and almost the same colour as the forest floor these well camouflaged little beauties can be very difficult to spot amongst leafy litter and decaying bracken. Once you've spotted your first mushroom, root your feet to the spot and simply scan the immediate area. Nine times out of ten you'll discover you've walked into a bountiful supply and once you've 'got your eye in' begin picking the largest mushrooms by snapping the stem just above ground level, as you would pick daisies. Leave the smaller fungi to grow on and continue their work.

How to prepare

Although the winter chanterelle appears quite delicate to look at, they are extremely absorbent and should only be gathered when conditions are relatively dry. To dry any surplus moisture from them, place somewhere cool on a clean dry dishcloth overnight, then gently brush off any debris and store in an open container in the fridge. Freshly picked, they can last for two to three weeks but fresh is best!

How to cook/use

This is one mushroom I don't bother picking to dry as it withers to nothing and doesn't reconstitute very well but when I do I combine reconstituted dried and freshly picked to make a winter chanterelle purée. The intense, earthy flavour is sumptuous but 3 kilos of fresh mushrooms reduce to only a few grams. If you have surplus have a go and see what you think.

FLOWER OF THE WOOD (ALSO CALLED GIROLLE & CHANTERELLE)

Cantharellus cibarius

Picking season: late June to November

Out in the forest one morning, I came across a mushroom gathering Italian acquaintance. As we approached each other he glanced at my rather large and full to overflowing wicker basket and sighed, "Ah, I see you have found the flower of the wood in good quantity this morning." I asked if this was a name the Italians used for this particular variety of delicious chanterelle and he replied very simply, "No, only me." He tipped his large-rimmed, felt hat and bade me farewell. As he continued on his way I watched the stick in his right hand lightly sweep the ground not missing any mushroom concealed by fallen leaves and resting on his left forearm was his enormous wicker basket. The scene reminded me of bygone days when similar baskets were filled with door-to-door deliveries of fresh bread straight from the baker and fresh butter was made with the first cream of the morning.

I, too, continued on my way through the forest looking for another patch of bright yellow chanterelles. It didn't take long but instead of just picking them I placed my basket on the forest floor and simply admired them. Almost instantly, I realised why my Italian friend had chosen his whimsical name, *Flower of the Wood*. The irregular shapes with their curved, wavy and lobed edges, some slightly fraying along with a small depression in the centre of each bright yellow cap, reminded me of leafless flowers growing out of the forest floor. From that day some thirty years ago, I too have referred to the chanterelle as 'flower of the wood.'

How to recognise

For identification purposes, unlike many other varieties of fungi, the chanterelle doesn't have a separate stem from its cap. The gills develop up from the stem and follow the curve of the underside of the head of the mushroom and also divide and fork as they extend toward the rim. The cap, stem and gills are bright yellow and, when split down the middle, their solid creamy white flesh can have a delicate apricot fragrance. The flesh is also unusually bug-free on the inside.

"These mushrooms are up in my top five and are simply delicious. Pictured above are two guests of THE PIG with their nice feed... very happy bunnies!"

Where to find

This early variety of mushroom can be found from late June onwards provided there is enough moisture retained in the forest floor. Most wild mushrooms have a preferred habitat such as under oak trees, on fallen beech trees or under protective leaf litter. Peculiarly, our little 'flower of the wood' can be found growing in all manner of places; beneath both deciduous and evergreen trees, mossy banks, along the side of ancient earthworks and ditches, so always keep your eyes peeled.

Being as brightly coloured as a buttercup they can be easily spotted in any woodland or forest. It's even possible to find small patches of chanterelles growing in unlikely places such as under holly bushes that have been grazed close to the forest floor by foraging animals. By early autumn, finding a feed becomes more difficult especially when they are growing amongst the bright yellow, fallen leaves of silver birch trees. At this time of the year you may have difficulty as Mother Nature's disguise is almost match perfect.

Collecting tips

When gathering chanterelles for a feed, take only the largest individual mushrooms and leave the smaller ones to grow on. Nip off the rooting end with a sharp knife and brush or blow away any leaf litter or dirt before placing them carefully in your basket.

Beware: the chanterelle has numerous look-a-likes. The false chanterelle (*Hygrophoropsis Aurantiaca*) grows mainly in coniferous woods in profuse quantities in some years and is more often a dirty, yellowy orange in colour. Its stem is considerably thinner than true chanterelles and is hollow at the root base. They can smell 'mushroomy' but with no hint of that fragrant apricot. They are said to be edible, but not by me!

How to prepare

Clean these mushrooms thoroughly as you pick them by cutting away the smallest amount of the dirty root-end and using a pastry brush or the brush end of a mushroom knife. Brush and blow away every little piece of debris before gently placing them in your basket. Using this on-the-spot cleaning method means you can get them in the pan even quicker. Should you opt for cleaning at home later you'll discover that the dirt and debris will take twice as long to remove and become a chore as it becomes engrained between the minute and fragile gills. Gritty mushrooms are 'yuk' in my dictionary. Your choice.

How to cook/use

I would not advise anybody to eat wild mushrooms raw. For beginners the safest way is to sauté freshly picked flower of the wood in exactly the same way as you would ceps or other varieties. Simply sauté them in a little olive oil and a knob of butter in a hot frying pan until they just begin to turn golden brown, then pop them onto fresh toasted bread and drizzle with the juices.

"My grandmother was Italian and my first memory of pickled mushrooms was plucking a few from the pan before she could get them into the jars. I still love them. Chanterelles lose everything if they dry out so this is the perfect way to preserve them to have on hand throughout the year."

A PINCH OF SALT COPPA SALAD
WITH PICKLED WINTER CHANTERELLE

Italian pickled wild mushrooms

Serves 4 as a starter

Equipment: sterilised kilner jars (see page 15)

1 kg wild chanterelles

250 ml water

250 ml white wine vinegar

4 garlic cloves

2 sprigs of thyme

3 cloves

5 juniper berries, (dried are fine)

1 tsp black peppercorns

½ tsp salt

2 bay leaves

500 ml olive oil, approximately

a few peppercorns, bay leaves & fresh thyme
for garnish

A *Pinch of Salt* coppa salad

Serves 4

150 g rocket, stemmed & washed

2 heads of chicory, separated into leaves

10 slices of *A Pinch of Salt* coppa, cut into thin
strips, or equivalent

10 semi-dried tomatoes, cut into thin strips

¼ red onion, very finely shaved

a few basil leaves, roughly torn

a handful of pine nuts, toasted

50 g pecorino shavings

For the dressing

3 tbsp extra virgin olive oil

1 tbsp red wine vinegar

1 pinch of ground nutmeg

salt & pepper

Italian pickled wild mushrooms

Yield: 2 500 ml jars

Carefully clean the mushrooms with a dry cloth making sure all detritus is removed.

In a saucepan, combine the water, vinegar, garlic, thyme, cloves, berries, peppercorns, salt and bay leaves, bring to the boil and add the mushrooms. With a spoon, immerse the mushrooms in the marinade. Cook for 3 minutes on high heat then reduce the heat and simmer for 10 minutes until the mushrooms are tender. Drain the mushrooms, allow to cool and then divide into sterilised jars. Add a few peppercorns, bay leaf and sprigs of thyme and fill the jars with olive oil making sure the mushrooms are completely covered. Seal and marinate in the refrigerator for 15 days before serving.

A *Pinch of Salt* coppa salad

At A Pinch of Salt we make our coppa in the traditional 'Parma capocollo' way using the muscle that runs between the neck and shoulder then air-dry it for 3 months and season it with cinnamon and fennel. It's delicate so it's a great addition to any salad.

In a salad bowl place the rocket, chicory, onion, coppa, tomatoes, basil, half the pine nuts and pecorino. Mix together the oil, vinegar, nutmeg, salt and pepper. Toss together with the salad ingredients. Scatter with the remaining pine nuts and pecorino and top generously with the pickled mushrooms.

HEDGEHOG MUSHROOMS

(ALSO CALLED PIED DE MOUTON)
Hydnum repandum

Picking season: September to December

Hedgehog mushrooms can be found growing as early as September but the best quality and quantity will not begin to grow until early October. The fallen leaves of autumn act as insulation against cooling temperatures and in a good hedgehog year, this hardy little fella can be gathered right through to the end of December in good quantities.

"Most chefs refer to them by their French name, pied de mouton or 'sheep's foot'."

How to recognise

It's solid and chunky with a large specimen growing up to 8 inches in diameter. Their pale, almost apricot pink-colour and spike-like gills give its quaint English name. When they first begin to grow their tops are more oval in shape with a small groove growing out from the stem and bear a good resemblance to the footprints of sheep.

"Pictured above, James' daughter Rio helps her dad gather some hedgehogs for lunch."

Where to find

The preferred habitat of hedgehog mushrooms is a mixture of deciduous and coniferous woods and they grow particularly well where there is good ground cover such as ferns and grasses. Although they're more difficult to find amongst this natural camouflage, they're usually in excellent condition having been so well protected from the elements.

The mycelium of the hedgehog lies hidden beneath the leaf mould of the forest floor and spreads and grows, in an invisible arc, unlike the fairy ring circle of many other varieties of fungus. When the mycelium produces the first fruiting bodies, they appear in the centre of the arc that lies hidden beneath the fallen leaves and twigs. Where there's no foliage to act as natural camouflage, these rainbow-shaped rows of mushrooms can be easily located, some as small as a metre or so long. During occasional exceptionally good hedgehog seasons, larger arcs can be ten metres or more long and can bear up to one hundred individual mushrooms varying in size with the largest growing in the centre of the arc and then decreasing in size as they spread in each direction along individual arc-shaped rows.

Collecting tips

Take a little extra care when gathering these beauties. They may look quite robust but are, in fact quite delicate and fragile. A sharp knife is essential. Simply slide your hand underneath the cap of the mushroom and locate the thick, fleshy stem between two fingers. Then, gently supporting the mushroom, slide the knife under your hand and sever the stem. Lift the mushroom away and place upside down in your basket making certain to leave the root in place as this variety of fungus is quite capable of producing another fruit body ready to harvest in another week or so.

Gathering hedgehogs has a downside that I feel compelled to share. When gathering your feed, your fingers will become heavily stained with the mushroom's henna-like dye. By the end of the day your fingers will look as though you're a heavy smoker. It takes some hefty scrubbing to remove. You've been warned!

How to prepare

Hedgehog mushrooms are a tasty variety that, like most others, are capable of absorbing lots of moisture so never wash them under a running tap and if you pick a feed after heavy rainfall, allow them to dry by storing them loosely on a tray in your fridge for a couple of days. Freshly picked and in prime condition, these mushrooms will last for two or even three weeks if stored correctly. The fleshy prickles should be gently scraped away and then simply brush the mushroom clean, finish by wiping with a damp cloth if necessary. Chefs always remove the prickly gills simply because they will fall away when cooking which will make a dish look messy.

How to cook/use

I would not advise anybody to eat wild mushrooms raw. For beginners the safest way is to sauté freshly picked hedgehog mushrooms in exactly the same way as you would ceps or other varieties. Simply sauté them in a little olive oil and a knob of butter in a hot frying pan until they just begin to turn golden brown, then pop them onto fresh toasted bread and drizzle with the juices.

HEDGEHOGS & OYSTER ON SOURDOUGH
WITH THREE-CORNERED GARLIC

Serves 2

400 g hedgehog & oyster mushrooms

1 garlic clove

2 tbsp vegetable oil

100 g butter

4 slices sourdough

a handful of edible flowers

a small bunch of flat-leaf parsley, chopped

salt & pepper

Heat the oil in a frying pan. Finely chop the garlic and cook without colour then add the mushrooms and sauté until golden brown. Add the butter and season to taste. Remove from the heat and stir in the parsley.

To serve, toast the sourdough and place in the centre of plates. Spoon the mushrooms onto the toast, drizzle with the leftover butter and top with wild edible flowers. Serve immediately.

(When Wildcook was photographed, hedgehog mushrooms were out of season so we just used wild oyster mushrooms. The result was just as yummy.)

"For me, wild mushrooms are the most beautiful things in the world. The feeling you get when you see them poking out of the ground is fantastic. There's nothing better than finding hedgehogs, getting them home and simply sautéing them in butter."

CRAB APPLES Malus sylvestris

Picking season: September to December
Extra Equipment: sometimes a garden rake could come in handy but I've never taken one!

The truly wild crab apple tree is the granddaddy of all of our cultivated varieties of edible apples including many of the lovely richly coloured flowering forms of ornamental crab apple trees found growing in many of our parks and gardens. The small fruit of the ornamentals differ, as they're oval shaped, more like rugby balls and vary in colour from bright yellowy-orange to cherry red but can be used in exactly the same way and make excellent amber coloured jelly.

How to recognise

A large crab apple tree can grow up to ten metres tall. The pretty pink flowers appear in May and are a delightful display against the electric green foliage of early spring but after the petals fall the crab apple becomes just another tree amongst so many others. As autumn approaches they stand out again as they shed their leaves to expose heavily laden crops of small golden fruit. The largest of these will grow to the size of golf balls but good spring weather will provide a higher yield of smaller fruit.

Where to find

The truly wild fruiting crab apple tree is deciduous and can be found growing in abundance in the south of England. Whilst it can be found just about anywhere in the UK it becomes less common the further north you travel. Crab apple trees thrive in moist, fertile soil and grow particularly well around the sunny edges and clearings of forests.

"Crab apple jelly is easy to make, as it's high in pectin; the natural heteropolysaccharide (that's sugar to you and me), the critical thickening agent in making jams and jellies. In fact, the pectin content can be so high that if you over boil the fruit your jelly will resemble a rubber ball. Who wants to spread that on their morning toast?"

Collecting tips

Crab apples are so bitter that forest animals consider them a last resort and usually only after they've been sweetened by winter frosts. Fallen fruit can be found literally covering the ground beneath the trees and only the harshest winter will see them all being eaten. If you're gathering from the forest floor select the best that haven't been nibbled by mice or trampled by ponies, cattle or deer. At best carefully pluck undamaged fruit that remain attached to the branches.

How to prepare

Wash the apples just a few at a time in a colander; rinse them thoroughly under a running cold tap. Job done.

How to cook/use

Generally, crab apples are used when processed and not as a raw ingredient. Most commonly they're used for making jelly either on their own or as a way to add zing when combined with blackberries and other fruits. They also make good cider and can be delicious when poached in sweet wine.

"This is an autumn dish. I love this time of year for the great seasonal produce and that the forest looks incredible with all the gold and red leaves and the excitement I experience when I stumble across something interesting to eat! I put this dish together using inspiration from the forest and my walled kitchen garden. You should be able to get most of these ingredients from your local butcher and delicatessen. I hope you enjoy cooking this dish as much as I enjoyed creating it."

NEW FOREST WOOD PIGEON & CRAB APPLE FRITTERS
WITH BEETROOT MASH, PENNY BUN & SLOE DRESSING

Serves 4 as a main
Equipment: food processor, fine sieve, deep-fryer

4 New Forest wood pigeons

Beetroot mash

6 potatoes, mashed (maris piper)

3 beetroot, cooked

150 ml double cream

50 g butter

salt & pepper

Crab apple fritters

2 medium crab apples

200 g corn flour

200 g strong flour

2 tsp bicarbonate of soda

iced sparkling water

12 large sage leaves

1½ - 3 litres rapeseed oil for deep-frying

Penny bun & sloe dressing

100 g fresh sloes

50 g caster sugar

1 large thick penny bun, sliced

a knob of garlic butter

a small bunch of parsley, chopped

For the beetroot mash, boil the potatoes in salted boiling water until cooked through. Purée the cooked beetroot in a food processor and pass both ingredients through a fine sieve.

Place in a mixing bowl and beat in the cream, butter and season to taste. Cover and keep warm until ready to serve.

For the pigeon, preheat oven to 180°C and season the pigeons with salt and pepper.

Sear the birds in a hot frying pan colouring all over before cooking in the oven for 12 minutes. When cooked leave to rest, covered for 6 minutes in a warm place.

For the crab apple fritters, preheat a deep-fryer to 180°C. Cut the crab apple into rings and remove the core, mix the corn flour, strong flour, bicarbonate of soda and sparkling water together and leave to rest for 10 minutes. When ready to serve, flour the apple rings and dip in the batter, deep-fry until golden and crispy. Deep-fry the sage leaves at the same time and thread through the centres of the apple ring.

For the penny bun and sloe dressing, cook the sloes and the sugar together over a medium heat until all the fruit has broken down and pass through a fine sieve. In a frying pan heat some oil and gently fry the mushrooms. When golden brown add the garlic butter and chopped parsley with a small drizzle of the sloe reduction.

To serve, assemble all the components on the plate whichever way you please. Be creative!

SWEET CHESTNUT Castanea sativa

Picking season: October to December
Extra equipment: a sturdy pair of gardening gloves, a stick and a basket

This deciduous hardwood tree is pretty hard to miss and can be found growing in parks and forests throughout the UK. The fruit of the English sweet chestnut tree is nothing like the size of the enormous Spanish varieties that you can forage from supermarkets. Believe me, our slightly smaller, English wild chestnuts make up for their diminished size with their succulent sweet flavour.

How to recognise

The chestnut tree has dark coarsely grooved bark and its leaves are pointed and oblong in shape, heavily veined on the underside with coarsely serrated edges like a woodman's saw. In July, when the trees are in full bloom, the creamy catkin-like flowers hang like long fingers and give off a heady aroma in the still morning air.

By late October the highly polished brown chestnuts fall and can be gathered in good quantities – that's if the squirrels, deer and other forest critters don't beat you to it. They're quite partial to a feast of wild chestnuts too!

Where to find

Sweet chestnut trees can be found growing in the wild where self-seeded saplings have spread over the years. The largest trees can grow similar in size and girth to giant beech trees though it's the smaller trees that produce the largest nuts. As with all fruiting trees and shrubs, always begin looking for them early in the season. Being able to recognise and identify the flowers before they fruit is vital and makes individual trees easy to spot when in full bloom. Chestnut trees come to full blossom from mid-July to early August.

It's a majestic tree and has been widely planted in parks as an ornamental and during autumn the fallen brown leaves lay a carpet that the child in all of us can't help but boisterously rustle through.

"The aroma, texture and flavour of freshly roasted sweet chestnuts are an essential part of every winter celebration."

Collecting tips

The nuts are protected by a spiky burr that's virtually impossible to penetrate with bare hands so arm yourself with a pair of gardening gloves, a good stick and a basket. Once you've located your tree, get to work using either your stick or the heal of your boot to scuff the prickly burrs until they break apart and give up the shiny brown kernels within. Eating the chestnuts raw is simply a waste of time and effort. While the outer brown shell is relatively easy to remove, the nut has a fleshy cream-coloured second skin that's bitter and a devil to pick off.

How to prepare

The unmistakable aroma of fresh roasting chestnuts always signals the onset of winter. While you can store freshly gathered wild chestnuts, the best flavour comes from roasting them soon after picking.

Preparation is simple. The shiny brown case of the nut shouldn't need washing; gently prick the skin with the point of a sharp knife without damaging the nut inside. This is essential as it stops the chestnuts exploding as they begin to cook.

How to cook/use

Raw chestnuts are dry and lack flavour but they transform when roasted over hot coals or in a heavy-based frying pan. When puréed they make a wonderfully earthy addition to soups, stews, stuffing and sauces. The purée also freezes well.

"For a bit of fun and texture I like to mix in a handful of chopped candied chestnuts into the ice cream."

CHESTNUT ICE CREAM & CANDIED CHESTNUTS

Serves 6 to 8 as a dessert
Equipment: ice cream maker

100 ml milk

300 g sweetened chestnut purée*

200 g icing sugar

12 egg yolks

2 to 4 tbsp dark or spiced rum

200 ml double cream

ice

2 to 3 candied chestnuts per serving

Candied chestnuts (marrons glacés)

450 g chestnuts, shelled

450 g granulated sugar

2½ c water

1 tsp vanilla extract

Put milk, chestnut purée and 150 g of the sugar in a saucepan and bring to the boil over medium heat. Whisk the egg yolks and the remaining sugar in a bowl to a ribbon consistency. Pour the boiling milk into the egg yolk mixture, whisking constantly, then pour it all back into the saucepan and stir over low heat until the mixture lightly coats the back of a wooden spoon. (When you run your finger through it, it should leave a clear path that stays on the spoon.) Remove from the heat immediately and pour the custard base into a bowl, add the rum and cool over ice, stirring occasionally to prevent a skin forming. When cold, pass the custard through a fine sieve and churn in an ice cream maker for 10 to 15 minutes. When the mixture is about halfway set, add the cream in a steady stream and churn for an additional 10 minutes until firm but still creamy.

Sweetened chestnut purée can be bought ready made. To make it from regular purée add approximately 50 to 75 g icing sugar to 415 g (1 tin) purée.

For the candied chestnuts, place the chestnuts in a large pan with just enough water to cover them. Bring the water to the boil for 10 minutes then drain and discard the cooking liquid. Using your fingers gently rub the thin skin off the cooked chestnuts.

In a separate pan, bring the water, granulated sugar and vanilla to the boil, stirring constantly for 5 minutes. Add the chestnuts to the sugar syrup and bring back to the boil, stirring constantly then continue to cook for a further 10 minutes. Pour the entire contents into a container, cover loosely and allow to marinate for 12 to 18 hours. Return the entire mixture to a clean pan and repeat the process, this time boiling for 2 minutes then allowing to marinate for a further 12 to 18 hours. Continue to repeat this process until the chestnuts have soaked up virtually all the sugar syrup.

Preheat an oven to 120°C, arrange the candied chestnuts on a parchment-lined baking sheet. Place the baking sheet into the oven and turn off the heat. Allow the chestnuts to dry in the oven for 45 minutes to 1 hour, until they have firmed up and the surfaces of the nuts are dry.

hop shoots

Contents

HORSERADISH
PICKLED WILD HORSERADISH

SLOES
SLOE GIN
SLOE GIN JAM

HAWTHORN
HAWTHORN PANNA COTTA

DAMSONS
DAMSON JELLY

BLACKBERRIES
BLACKBERRY SORBET

DOG ROSE HIPS
DOG ROSE TURKISH DELIGHT

Hedgerow harvest

HEDGEROW HARVEST

Harvesting wild edible goodies from hedgerows is just as rewarding as finding a basketful of wild mushrooms and, like mushroom picking, you'll quickly establish your favourite patches.

Long before the age of barbed wire the simple hedgerow wasn't quite so simple. They served two main purposes; one as a territorial boundary but more importantly hedgerows had to be dense and impenetrable containing pasture for grazing animals. Before the advent of modern day farming and even when I was a young lad the Old English countryside was a unique landscape of small patchwork fields.

With spring in the air, from April onwards, flowering shrubs and bushes begin to burst into life. Busy bees and other insects get to work, gathering their own crop in exchange for pollinating the countless blooms that will become autumn fruit, from blackberries and sloes to hawberries and hops.

It is in autumn that hedgerows really come into their own. They simply burst with an abundance for you to pick and enjoy. Once the final fruits of sloe, rose hip, damson and haw ripen and fall, the near-naked winter branches reveal the splendour of colourful lichens that cling to them like delicate lingerie. By late March the opening buds of spring will once again fully clothe the bushes hiding these pretty lichens under dense green foliage protecting these frail underthings from heat and dehydration.

Safety: Always check area bylaws & gain landowners permission before gathering.

Standard equipment: wellies, sturdy walking shoes or boots, thorn-proof gloves, kitchen scissors and plenty of plastic containers.

HORSERADISH Armoracia Rusticana

Picking season: Year-round
Extra equipment: Spade

Mention horseradish and most people instantly conjure up an image of roast beef and Yorkshire pudding and then, almost unbelievably, they go to the supermarket and buy horseradish sauce in a jar when the real thing can be found growing in abundance almost anywhere around the entire UK.

How to recognise

Horseradish has large, broad, bright green leaves with tall spikes of insignificant small white flowers and a massive root system. The extracted root can be likened to an extremely knobbly and wiry parsnip and is also similar in colour. Many of you may have probably seen horseradish but easily have mistaken it for the very large dock leaf. Once you have found this quite handsome plant, making the all important positive identification is very easy by simply crushing the leaves to release the instant aroma of fresh horseradish; it will immediately excite the taste buds.

Where to find

The poorer the soil, the more horseradish seems to flourish and the large leaved plants can be found growing in the most unexpected areas from roadside verges, along the edges of footpaths and riverbanks to meadows and even wasteland. Horseradish is a perennial weed and will self-seed and spread at a remarkable pace, which is absolutely fine by me.

Collecting tips

To extract enough of the root for your own use, the first thing you need is the landowner's permission or simply do as I do and grow your own which will give you a year round fresh supply. The distorted taproots grow deep so you will need either a garden spade or a decent sized sharp knife. Scrape or dig away the soil from the base of the plant and sever the root as deep as is possible – six to eight inches below the surface will be sufficient and give you a sizable amount of root which will make the hottest, tangiest fresh horseradish sauce you will ever taste.

"Call me old fashioned but I like to keep a generous jar in the fridge and add a dollop of freshly whipped cream for Sunday roast."

How to prepare

Rinse the root in cold tap water to loosen any ingrained soil and then give it a good scrub under a running tap using a washing up brush. Your knobbly root should polish up quite nicely, however, if the root you have extracted is particularly disfigured you may need to cut it into slightly smaller pieces in order to remove any debris from the many crevices. At this stage, the skin of your fresh horseradish root should be pearly white and ready to use. You can peel away skin but I prefer to leave it intact. Grate the root as finely as you desire – I use a hand wound parmesan grater. Simply cut the root into chunks the size of hen's eggs and grate them into a clean bowl. Always grate at arm's length to avoid the onion effect on your eyes as horseradish contains pungent oil that gives the finished sauce that amazing zap.

How to cook/use

Horseradish is so versatile. It can be used raw, grated into salads or onto vegetables such as beetroot or into mashed potatoes. A few grated shreds are a great addition to a refreshing glass of tomato juice or Bloody Mary and it can add a zingy kick to Mary Rose sauce for a prawn cocktail.

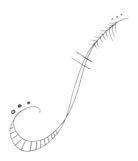

PICKLED WILD HORSERADISH

Yield: condiment for 6 to 8
Equipment: sterilised kilner jar *(see page 15)*

30 g wild horseradish root, peeled & grated

2 tbsp white wine vinegar

a generous pinch of English mustard powder

a generous pinch of caster sugar

salt & pepper

To serve

150 ml double cream, lightly whipped

Soak the grated horseradish in 4 tbsp hot water for 30 minutes. Drain away the excess moisture then mix in the vinegar, mustard and sugar. Check the seasoning and balance with a touch more sugar if needed and season to taste. This mixture can be stored in a sealed, sterilised jar in the fridge for several weeks.

To make a creamed sauce, lightly whip some double cream and stir in pickled horseradish to a thick consistency. Check seasoning before serving.

"If you don't have wild horseradish to hand this recipe works equally well for the garden variety. It's a perfect partner for beef or roasted beetroot."

SLOES (BLACKTHORN) Prunus spinosa

Picking season: October to December
Extra equipment: lots of enthusiasm, long sleeves to protect from thorns

This deciduous shrub's Latin name is *Prunus Spinosa*. Technically it's a blackthorn bush and is, as its name suggests, a descendant of the prune. The hard little fruits can't be eaten like prunes or plums though, as their flavour is so harsh it's worse than sucking lemons. They're so bitter they instantly dry out the mouth causing excessive salivation.

Blackthorn is gnarly and knotted hardwood most commonly used for making walking and hiking sticks. Blackthorn was also used for making farm tools and implements.

How to recognise

Sloes are the fruit of the blackthorn. They're marble-sized, blue-black hard little fruits coated with a pale blue powder that rubs off when picked.

The sloe harvest begins in October and as autumn temperatures fall the foliage drops to unveil hidden treasure. A fully laden bush can look almost blue as the ripening fruit replaces the foliage of this hardy shrub.

Where to find

Blackthorn is quite an unremarkable looking shrub that can be found growing just about anywhere in UK hedgerows, woodland and forest, but grows particularly well amongst hedgerows, meadows and scrubland. It is pretty unattractive for most of the year but just for a few weeks, from mid-March onwards the whole bush bursts into life when the leafless branches are covered with tiny, snow-white clusters of flowers.

The blackthorn bush always blooms at this time of year, but in greater profusion when there is a cold snap in the weather – this is known as a *Blackthorn Winter* amongst older country folk. When in full bloom, the bushes can be easily spotted as the profusion of flowers transforms these naked shrubs for a week or so giving insects an essential and hefty job of cross-pollination.

Collecting tips

These tough skinned fruits also need a frost or two before they are picked in order to soften them sufficiently to coerce them to release their tart juice. Whilst out in the forest gathering mushrooms in early October if, by chance, I happen to come across a blackthorn bush with a particularly heavy crop of plump, dusty fruit, then a carrier bagful containing a couple of kilos will be tied to the handle of my mushroom basket. Be careful as the thorns are particularly sharp and it's advisable to wear gloves when harvesting. An early frost can be replicated easily by freezing the fruit overnight. This softens the skin to perfection allowing the sloes to release their juice that gives sloe gin or vodka that 'kick like a mule' flavour.

How to prepare

Sloes are unpalatable to fruit-eating insects such as flies and wasps. I'm happy to use the freshly picked fruits that have been washed by rainfall but feel free to wash yours under a running cold tap if you wish.

How to cook/use

When most us think of sloes we automatically think of sweet sloe gin but believe me vodka, whiskey, brandy even sherry make great alternatives. An individual sloe is almost seventy five per cent stone covered by a thin layer of olive green, juicy, astringent flesh. Quite surprisingly, this makes a delicious tasting jelly that goes particularly well with meats, such as lamb, goose or duck.

"When I was a nipper there was nothing more fun, if mischievous, than a y-shaped blackthorn branch to use as a catapult. My mates and I used to get up to all sorts! Fortunately, blackthorn catapulting has lost its appeal over the years."

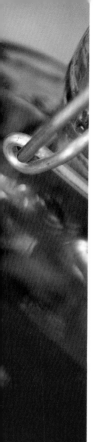

SLOE GIN

Yield: 2 litres
Equipment: 5 litre demijohn or sealable plastic container, fine sieve, 4 ½ litre sterilised sealable bottles *(see page 15)*

900 g sloes, stalks removed

2 litres good quality gin or vodka

500 ml simple syrup, approximately, *(see page* 192)

Place freshly picked sloes in the freezer overnight. This replaces the need to prick each berry with a pin. Pour the sloes and spirit into a demijohn and leave in a dark, cool place. Gently turn the demijohn upside down and back a few times after 2 to 3 days then again every week for one month then every 2 to 3 weeks for another 3 or 4 months at least. As time progresses, have a little taste and judge when the taste of the berry has reached its full potential (this could take even several months longer). Another good indicator will be the depth of the colour.

When ready, pass the liquid through a fine sieve into a large heavy-bottomed pan. Set the sloes aside. Heat to warm, just below simmer and start to add small amounts of simple syrup tasting after each addition to desired sweetness. (Remember that once bottled the sugar will intensify with age so be careful.) Strain into sterilised, sealable bottles.

"Making good quality infused spirits is really quite simple.
It just takes a little patience. For special celebrations I serve
sloe kir royale – sloe gin and champagne!"

SLOE GIN JAM

Yield: approximately 2 litres
Equipment: fine muslin, sterilised kilner jars
(see page 15)

900 g sloes, reserved from making gin

1.8 kg cooking apples, washed & chopped

apple cider

juice and zest of 2 small lemons

granulated sugar

a knob of butter

Place the sloes in a large heavy-bottomed pan. Add just enough cider to cover the fruit, bring to the boil and simmer until the berries are pulpy (you may need to mash them a bit).

Add the apples and lemon juice and zest. Bring to the boil, simmer until pulpy again, and leave to cool down a bit. Strain the pulp through a fine muslin into a suitable container overnight. (Don't be tempted to squeeze the bag to rush this process. Let it press slowly to produce a clear liquid.)

The next day, measure the juice and add 400 g of sugar per 500 ml. Bring to the boil and stir over medium heat skimming off any scum as it collects on the surface. Add the butter and boil until the liquid reaches setting point. 'The ripple test' is the simplest and best method to check for setting point. Simply drop a little jam onto a chilled saucer. Let it cool a little then push your finger through the jam. If the jam parts leaving wrinkled ripples, it is ready.

"When it comes to sustainability this is one of the best uses of a byproduct. There's no waste and a tasty result."

HAWTHORN Crataegus monogyna

Picking season: April to November
Extra equipment: long sleeves to protect from thorns

The hawthorn with its thorny impenetrable foliage is a common sight throughout the UK and for centuries has been used as the backbone of hedgerow construction. Hawthorn is actually a small tree and when left to its own devices, can grow to fifteen metres or more. In early spring freshly picked youngest green shoots are a welcome addition to any salad bowl and the delicate flavour of the blossom can make a fragrant spring syrup or bring a floral hint to panna cotta or any cream dessert. The fruit of the hawthorn is always abundant though not widely used. It makes an interesting addition to jams, preserves and chutneys.

"If you can't find a hawthorn bush then give up foraging and join the Ramblers! Hawthorn is probably one of the most common hedgerow plants."

How to recognise

The easiest way to distinguish hawthorn from blackthorn is simple – and very interesting if, like me, you're into this sort of thing. To the untrained eye or at a glance, the two look quite similar. It's a simple matter of timing. The blackthorn flowers before the leaves begin to open – their profuse clusters of small white flowers popping out against the stark woody bramble, whereas the hawthorn is totally the opposite, it bursts into bloom after the leaves have fully opened so the flowers are surrounded by shrouds of green – simple as that.

During the late summer and into the autumn the two plants become unmistakable with the dusty-blue marble-sized blackthorn sloes and the smaller smartie-sized fruit of the hawthorn that glows ruby red when ripe for the picking.

Where to find

The funny thing is not many people even realise that the leaves, blossoms and fruit are all edible. The soft ripened fruit is always plentiful and a main sustenance through harsh winter months for birds such as redwings and fieldfares – they love 'em.

Collecting tips

When collecting a few spring hawthorn leaves for your salad bowl, only gather a few from individual bushes and pinch out the young buds with your thumb and forefinger. Only gather the youngest budding shoots, as they are by far the tastiest. Once the leaves have been open for a couple of days they harden and their texture becomes almost papery – certainly not fit for the salad bowl.

To gather the flower heads, simply nip the florets off with a pair of kitchen scissors. For the best flavour only gather the flowers that are just beginning to open – if the petals are falling they're past their sell by date and should be left to develop into autumn fruit.

In autumn the berries ripen to perfection after a few frosts. Bright red in colour these squishy berries have a similar texture to fruity peanut butter. When gathering a feed it's nearly impossible to avoid getting stabbed by the profusion of sharp thorns that adorn this shrub cum tree so cover up and take time to locate a bush with larger berries and leave the small fruit for the birds' winter dining.

How to prepare

The flower heads should be used straight from the bush. Any attempt to wash them will just wash away the delicate flavour.

The berries can be washed thoroughly in a colander under cold running tap water.

How to cook/use

The budding shoots are always an interesting addition to a spring salad and can also be used as sandwich filler, in place of lettuce.

The flower heads can be used to make a simple infused syrup for flavouring drinks and jellies, or used in the same way as you might use honey. I leave winemaking to the experts and enthusiasts but in days gone by hawflower wine was quite the thing.

Eaten raw the ripe fruit can be described as more 'interesting' than amazing, but what our little hawberries lack in flavour they really do make up for with their natural vitamin C content. They become more interesting when blended with crab apples and they're a great addition to chutneys.

HAWTHORN PANNA COTTA
WITH WILD BLACKBERRIES & COULIS

Serves 6
Equipment: fine sieve, blender, chilled glasses
or dariole moulds

several large scoops of hawthorn flowers

3 gelatine leaves

250 ml milk

250 ml double cream

100 g sugar

1 tsp vanilla extract

Blackberry coulis

125 g wild blackberries
   (save a few for garnishing)

1 tsp sugar

3 tbsp water

a few edible forget-me-nots for decoration

For the panna cotta, soak the gelatine leaves in cold water until soft. Combine the milk, cream, sugar and vanilla in a heavy-bottomed pan and warm to just simmering. Remove excess water from the gelatine and stir into the cream mixture until completely dissolved. Add as many of the hawthorn flowers as the mixture will hold. While keeping the mixture warm, stir gently with a wooden spoon frequently enough to keep it from thickening on the sides for about 1 hour. (The longer you allow the mixture to infuse the stronger the flavour.) When ready, strain through a fine sieve and pour into glasses or moulds. Refrigerate until set.

For the coulis, purée the blackberries, sugar and water in a blender. Pass through a fine sieve and set in the fridge until ready to use.

When ready to serve, cover the panna cotta with a thin layer of coulis, crush on a few blackberries and decorate with edible flowers.

If using moulds, release the panna cottas by setting them briefly in warm water then carefully joggle them out. If they prove to be a bit stubborn, carefully run a sharp knife around the edge.

"This easy pudding is simplicity in a glass with a taste of the wild."

DAMSONS Prunus insititia

Damsons aren't as common as they used to be in wild hedgerows but a great bonus if you can find them. Although larger, they're identical in shape and colour to sloes, the fruit of the blackthorn bush and directly related – probably an ancestor. Just like their smaller cousins they taste rather astringent when eaten before fully ripened but a couple of frosts transform them into something sweet and delicious unlike sloes that retain their bitterness with or without the frost.

How to recognise

Damsons are shrubs that can grow to be as large as trees. They're far less prickly than blackthorn bushes so are easier to cultivate. Where sloes bloom in clusters of white flowers, damsons have five-petalled white flowers that grow singly allowing individual fruits room to fatten as they ripen. Where a typical sloe is marble-sized, damsons grow twice as large.

Where to find

Damsons were once highly favoured in hedgerow construction for their dense wood and weather resistant hardiness. As a unique fruit to the UK, it has always been popular, so much so that it became a cultivated orchard crop. So if you find *your* wild damson bush protect its whereabouts as if it were your favourite porcini spot.

"Nowadays its easier to find them in garden centres and neighbours, gardens than in the hedgerow."

Collecting tips

When out gathering any type of fruit I always take an old wooden 'Charlie Chaplin' type walking stick, the reason being that you can almost guarantee the best pickings will always be just out of reach, so with the aid of the crook end of the stick, your basket will be filled much more quickly and easily. Pick the damsons one at a time and place the ripe fruits carefully in your waiting basket.

How to prepare

Wash your ripe, juicy damsons in a colander under cold running tap water. Done. The fruit can also be stored in the freezer and when making preserves, the stones can be removed more easily after cooking.

How to cook/use

When fully ripe, damsons are simply divine eaten freshly picked from the bush. They're traditionally used for making preserves – jams, jellies, compotes and even marmalade and are also delicious when added to savoury sauces and meat dishes. History also tells us that they were used to create dyes for wool and linen and today, like sloes, are frequently used as an infusion for cordials and spirits such as gin and vodka.

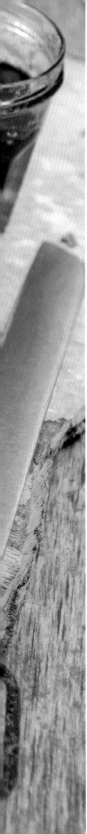

DAMSON JELLY

Yield: approximately 2 litres
Equipment: jam pan or deep heavy-bottomed
pan, fine muslin, sterilised kilner jars
(see page 15)

1.8 kg damsons, stalks removed

1.4 kg cooking apples, chopped
 (not peeled or cored)

juice of half a lemon

granulated sugar
 (450 g for every 600 ml juice)

2.85 litres good English cider

a knob of butter

Put the fruit in a large jam pan and cover with the cider. Simmer until soft and pulpy then transfer to muslin jelly bag or cloth, seal tightly and hang over a bowl to strain overnight. Make sure the bowl is large enough to catch the juice and don't be tempted to push the fruit through the cloth or you'll end up with cloudy jelly.

Next day, put 3 to 4 small plates in the freezer for testing the jelly and sterilise the jars. Measure the fruit extract and pour back into the clean jam pan. Add the sugar and gently heat until the sugar has completely dissolved then add the lemon juice. (If the sugar isn't completely dissolved the jelly will crystalise.) Bring to the boil for 10 minutes, skim the scum that forms and be careful not to boil over. Remove the jelly from the heat to test.

To test that the jelly has reached the setting point, put a teaspoon of jelly on one of the cold plates from the freezer and leave to cool. If the jelly is ready it crinkles when pushed with your finger. If the jelly does not crinkle place back on the heat and boil for a further ten minutes then test again. When ready, stir in a knob of butter and remove any leftover scum.

Fill the sterilised jars to the very top, as the liquid will reduce slightly as it cools. Allow to cool then seal and keep in a cool dry place. Once opened keep refrigerated. The jelly is ready to use but will keep for several months.

"This jelly is great with just about everything from toast or oatmeal at breakfast to a sweet topping on rice pudding."

BLACKBERRIES (BRAMBLE BUSH) Rubus fruiticosus

Picking season: August to October
Extra equipment: a walking stick is quite handy

The shiny, fresh fruit of the bramble bush is the delectable blackberry and is almost certainly one of the few wild foods used by our hunter-gatherer ancestors that most, if not all of us, have at one time or other plucked from a bush and eaten while out walking.

The whole plant is a mass of prickles with the stems having the largest thorns. These can easily be snapped off between your thumb and finger. Even the stems and leaves have small prickles and the underside of the palmate leaves contain minute and needle-sharp prickles. All in all, it's practically impossible to gather blackberries without the laughter being punctuated with the occasional 'ouch' but, as I tell the children, 'It's not like being bitten by a shark!'

How to recognise

The bramble bush flowers from May onwards and produces one of nature's prettiest wild flowers. Each flower has five fragile petals that can range in colour from the palest pink to almost purple. The flower clusters attract an army of bugs that help pollination, ensuring a good crop of plump, shiny berries from as early as mid-August through September and even the early part of October providing the weather stays relatively dry.

Where to find

Bramble bushes are abundant throughout the UK and can spread at an alarming rate. Any sprouting stem that shoots up but cannot find another plant to support its growth will eventually bend and touch the ground, the tip will then simply root and sprout fresh growth in an everlasting advance. Hedgerows along footpaths and country lanes are ideal and will usually provide the best and cleanest pickings.

"If like me you're a bit of a kid at heart, use a small amount of spit to stick them on your nose; the sight of a prickle-sprouted nose always makes children laugh and before you can say Peter Pan everyone has a prickly nose and a jolly fit of giggles."

Collecting tips

Blackberry picking is still a great family pursuit and as long as everybody knuckles down and doesn't eat too many while picking, a few kilos can soon be gathered. If you're gathering for jam-making, always pick a few of the slightly plum-red unripe berries as they contain more pectin that is essential in making jam set.

A stick with a crook or old walking stick is an ideal tool for reaching the prickly branches that are just out of reach. These always seem to have the plumpest and shiniest fruit. The upside down walking stick can also be very useful for pushing the prickly stems away when you are moving around the bushes, thus avoiding too many minor scratches.

If you're gathering blackberries in a quiet, undisturbed and sunny area, always be aware and keep your eyes peeled for any snakes, especially the venomous adder or viper. They can be easily recognised by the dark zigzag stripe down their back. Although attack is their last form of defence, they will strike if startled, especially if you accidentally place a foot too close to a sleeping snake while you are quietly manoeuvring yourself around a bush. Snakes are cold-blooded and regularly sunbathe in order to maintain their body temperature but don't let my warning put you off – you'll be privileged to see one. Vibrations of approaching footfall are usually enough for any snake to slither off to another quiet and sunny spot, usually next to a bush covered in even more juicy blackberries!

How to prepare

Tip just a handful at a time into a large plastic colander and gently roll around under cold running water for just a few seconds. Washing too many for too long will see the berries disintegrate and lose their flavour. All you need to do is quickly rinse and pat dry making sure any tiny critters or detritus have been removed.

How to cook/use

Blackberries are bundles of mouth-watering joy and endlessly useful. Classic jams and conserves – especially with crab apples are a must in any forager's larder. They're perfect with savoury dishes such as venison and game but for me, I love to munch a few as I wander down the path.

BLACKBERRY SORBET

Serves 4
Equipment: fine sieve, ice cream maker

400 g blackberries

375 g caster sugar

300 ml water

juice of half a lemon

4 tsp liquid glucose

1 tbsp water

75 g caster sugar

To prepare the sorbet mixture place 300 g sugar, water, lemon juice and liquid glucose into a pan over a low heat. Stir the mixture and slowly bring to the boil for 5 minutes, then remove from the heat and place into the fridge to chill.

For the blackberries, place the blackberries, 75 g sugar and water into a clean pan over low heat and cook gently to soften the fruit. Pass through a sieve into a bowl. Add the the chilled syrup and churn in an ice cream maker according to manufacturer's instructions. Transfer to a freezer-proof container and freeze until needed.

"I've never come home from picking blackberries without my arms covered in scrapes but the end result of this sorbet is worth every scratch."

DOG ROSE HIPS Rosa canina

For me, from mid-May onward, the sight of the first exquisite blooms of wild or dog rose is just as beautiful as seeing the first Brimstone butterfly of early spring – and the two together are stunningly beautiful.

The bright red hips that ripen in late autumn are actually the seedpods of the delicate pink blossoms. The wall or flesh of the hip is only a millimetre or so thick and contains an amazing concentration of vitamin C. In the 1940's, aware of this abundant natural vitamin source, *The Ministry of Food* supported a national gathering campaign to help feed WWII servicemen and their families at home. They were gathered by the ton for the production of rose hip syrup. The syrup contained a concentration of vitamin C twenty times stronger than oranges and with food rationing in place the demand for the humble rose hip skyrocketed.

The nation pulled together and every autumn an army of volunteers gathered tons and tons of rose hips. Rose hip syrup was widely available and taken as a tonic for everything. It was standard practice to give children one or two spoonfuls per day ensuring their essential daily dose of vitamin C. As a young boy in the 50's, I was given this very same treatment and rose hip syrup was still widely available through the 60's. If you fancy giving it a try one kilo of freshly picked rosehips yields one litre of syrup and it's far easier than making jam or jelly.

How to recognise

From late spring onward this straggling deciduous shrub is a complete tangle of shoots. Every shoot is armed with countless hooked prickles and the pinnate leaves form in two or three pairs along the central stem with a solitary leaf at the end. In full bloom the dog rose becomes a mass of fragile pink flowers, each with five floppy delicate petals that easily detach from their honey-gold centre. These stamen-filled centres are plentiful to ensure a good crop of bright-red oval-shaped hips in autumn.

Where to find

Dog rose is common and can be found growing throughout the UK. It thrives along hedgerows and scrubland, around the fringes of woodland and amongst bushes in un-grazed meadowland. Left unattended they become an impenetrable prickly bramble easily spotted in late spring by their masses of pretty pale pink flowers.

Collecting tips

Rose hips should be snapped from their stem; if you attempt to pull the hips you'll find yourself tangled in the mass of prickly, whip-like branches. Alternatively, use sharp scissors and snip the hips off just below the fruit. The same rule applies to rose hips as sloes from the blackthorn bush and they should only be gathered after a frost or two. The only difference is that hardly anybody gathers rose hips these days so if you happen to find a bush covered in shiny red hips during September, they're likely safe to leave to ripen and soften naturally. However, the old 'overnight in the freezer' trick is more reliable than anticipating a frost allowing you to gather from September onward.

As with most fruits you've got to work fast making your syrup as soon as possible. If the rose hips are left lying around, they'll lose the vitamin C for which they're so highly prized.

One last thing, in the interests of nature, when gathering a few petals, never pick whole flowers; the best way to collect the delicate pink petals is to gently tap the branches and let them fall into a basket – more than enough petals can be gathered quite easily without harming the plant and will allow future hips to form.

How to prepare

If you are going to make dog rose tea with the leaves, rinse them under a running cold tap. The petals should only be gathered when they're ready to fall, gently tap the prickly stems to release the petals and use these freshly picked; the hips on the other hand should be rinsed in a colander under cold running water.

A word of warning

Never attempt to eat rose hips freshly picked or whole. On the inside of the hips there are a number of seeds, each seed is covered in minute sharp hairs that, if swallowed, can be a dangerous irritant as they pass through your system. I have never swallowed the seeds to find out how uncomfortable they are but I can assure you one rose hip ingested or dropped down the back of a shirt could cause mayhem. Don't try it.

How to cook/use

Dog rose leaves can be used dried or freshly picked to make a delicate tea and is well worth trying. The flower petals are also edible, and with their faintly perfumed flavour and pale pink fragility, they can make a salad or dessert look amazing. Simply sprinkle a few on ice cream then drizzle rose hip syrup over the top.

The hardship of war has given us some of our most treasured dishes and ingredients. Rose hip syrup is one of those all-British staples. It's perfect as a simple drink with hot water; for a fussy little one to help top up vitamin intake; as a dessert on ice cream, with yoghurt, porridge, whatever you fancy.

"The flavour of homemade rose hip syrup can't be matched by store-bought."

DOG ROSE TURKISH DELIGHT

Yield: 40-ish 2.5 cm pieces
Equipment: sugar thermometer, silpat tray or parchment, ½ litre sterilised kilner bottle
(see page 15)

8 gelatine leaves

500 g granulated sugar

a few drops of rosewater

a few drops of pink liquid food colouring

2 tbsp icing sugar

1 tbsp corn flour

18 cm square cake tin

Pure distilled rose water

Yield: approximately ½ litre
Equipment: deep, heavy-bottomed pan with curved lid, a small brick, a pyrex or heat resistant bowl that sits easily inside the pan, sterilised ½ litre bottle (see page 15)

rose petals, enough to fill 6 to 7 pint glasses
   (make sure they haven't been sprayed with
   chemicals)

water (amount depends on quantity of petals)

a large bag of ice cubes

*"As a Turkish delight lover
I think this is a perfect end
to a wild meal."*

Pour 300 ml water into a pan and add the gelatine leaves and leave to soften for a few minutes then place the pan on low heat and stir until the gelatine completely dissolves then add the sugar and stir until it has dissolved. Increase the heat and bring the mixture to the boil, reduce the heat and simmer gently for 20 mins.

Remove the pan from the heat and stir in the rose water and food colouring, until it's pale pink. If you don't have a silpat tray, line a cake tin with parchment, then pour in the mixture and leave in a cool place to set overnight.

Sift the icing sugar and corn flour together and generously dust a clean work surface. Ease the set jelly out of the tin onto the sugar and using a damp, clean long-bladed knife cut the jelly into 2.5 cm cubes making sure to clean and dampen the blade between each cut. Coat all cut surfaces in the sugar mixture.

Place in a container lined with parchment, in a single layer, dust with a little extra sugar and keep in a cool, dry place (but not in the fridge) for up to 1 week.

For the rose water, place the brick in the center of the pan and the bowl on top and surround with the rose petals so they reach to just about the top. Pour in just enough water to cover the petals, which should be just above the brick.

Place the lid of the pan upside down and bring to the boil. Reduce the heat to low, when it begins to simmer load the inverted lid with ice. This creates a distilling process. As the water evaporates it reaches the cold top and drains back into the bowl. Every 20 minutes or so quickly lift the lid, check the amount of remaining water in the petals and extract the pure rose water from the bowl. Repeat the process until you have distilled the water without burning the pan. Pour the liquid into sterilised bottles and store in a dark, cool place.

hedge garlic

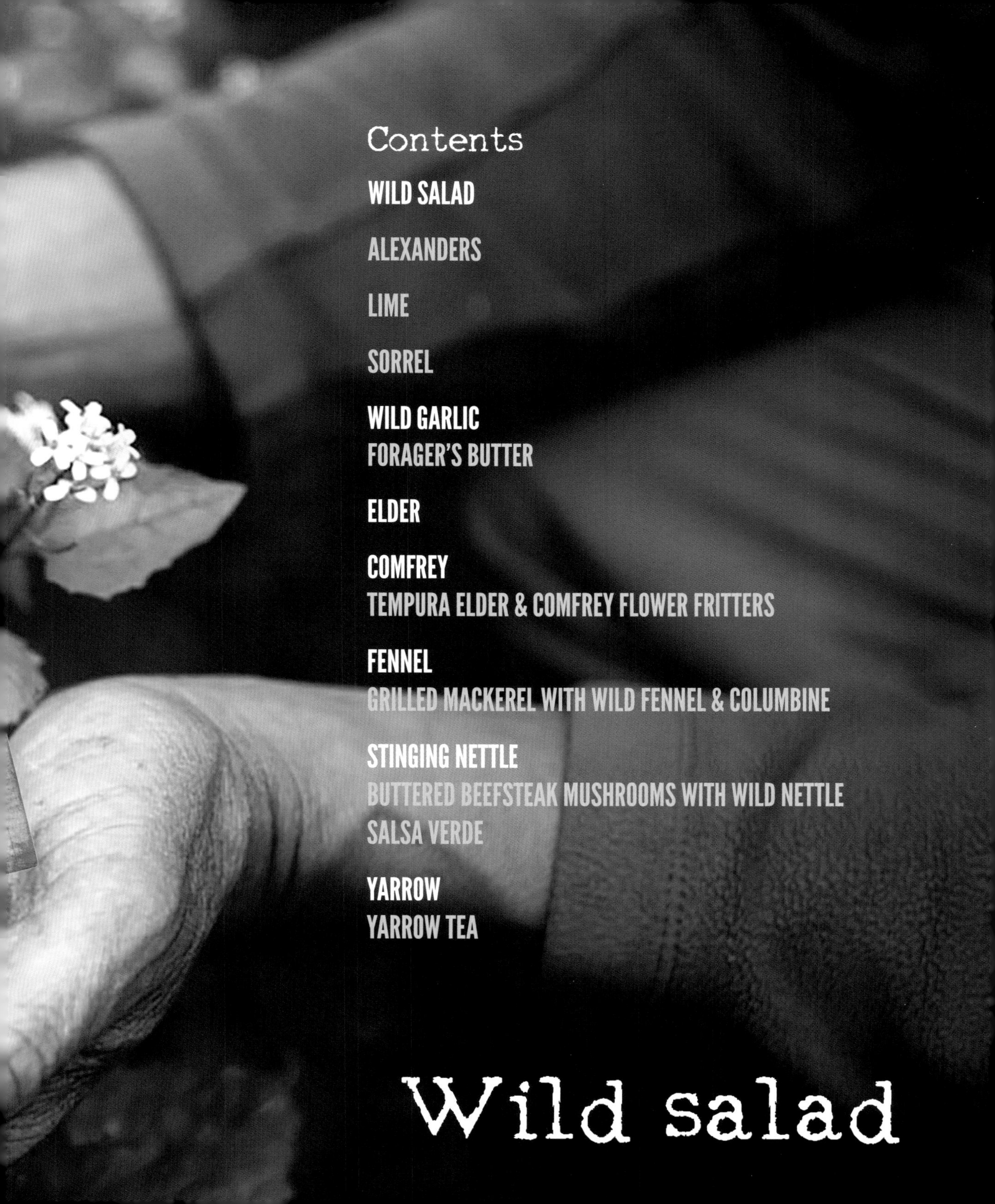

Contents

WILD SALAD

ALEXANDERS

LIME

SORREL

WILD GARLIC
FORAGER'S BUTTER

ELDER

COMFREY
TEMPURA ELDER & COMFREY FLOWER FRITTERS

FENNEL
GRILLED MACKEREL WITH WILD FENNEL & COLUMBINE

STINGING NETTLE
BUTTERED BEEFSTEAK MUSHROOMS WITH WILD NETTLE
SALSA VERDE

YARROW
YARROW TEA

Wild salad

WILD SALAD

Picking green things can be just as dangerous as picking wild mushrooms, there are a great many plants growing in the wild that are poisonous. A plant may look green and succulent but that doesn't make it an instant addition to any salad bowl. 100% positive identification is paramount and the most important foraging rule whether you're gathering wild salad, mushrooms, fruits, nuts or berries.

From early April through to the end of June gathering a colander full of incredible wild salad leaves can be extremely easy. Once you've identified and sampled their delights you'll wonder exactly why you've been buying cellophane bags of prepared salad leaves for so long.

Throughout spring and early summer the mind-blowing array of different tastes and textures are amazing and soon will see you selecting your personal favourite tasty weeds to add to your salad mix. Salad is basically just green stuff and I always say that a salad is only as good as the dressing that makes it come to life.

Safety: always check area bylaws and obtain permission from landowners.

Standard equipment: wellies, gathering basket, kitchen scissors, garden gloves, colander, spray bottle for water, salad spinner.

WILD SALAD

Picking season: almost year-round and varies by species

From April onwards, gathering a colander full of incredible wild salad leaves is as easy as a gentle walk in the country. The varieties are endless but here are a few of my favourites. Once you've sampled their delights you'll wonder why you've been buying your salad in plastic bags all these years.

Alexanders (*Smyrnium olusatrum*)
Beech (*Fagus sylvatica*)
Bittercress (*Cardamine hirsuta*)
Chickweed (*Stellaria media*)
Chives (*Allium schoenoprasum*)
Daisy (*Bellis perennis*)
Dandelion (*Taraxacum officinale*)
Dog rose (*Rosa canina*)
Hawthorn (*Crataegus monogyna*)
Lady's smock (*Cardamine pratensis*)
Lime or linden (*Tilia family*)
Sorrel (*Rumex acetosa*)
Sowthistle (*Sonchus arvensis*)
Wild garlic/ramsons (*Allium ursinum*)
Hedge garlic (*Alliaria petiolata*)
Wood sorrel (*Oxalis acetosella*)

How to recognise

Most wild salad leaves are relatively small when compared to the large cultivated varieties that are widely available in most supermarkets but what they lack in size they more than make up for with a mind-blowing array of textures and delicate flavours that can really excite the taste buds.

Where to find

From early spring most hedgerows, foreshores, meadow land, parks, gardens and even your own lawn and garden borders can all contain enough goodies to pick an amazing collection of wild salad bits and pieces. Always make certain to gather your plants well away from any form of pollution such as roadside verges and farmland where pesticides may have been used and *never* gather anything you intend to eat close to where people walk their dogs!

"I always say that good dressing brings a salad to life so James has included great ideas for dressings and a few more nifty concoctions."

Collecting tips

My preferred method of picking is with my fingers straight into a medium-sized colander, mixing the salad as I go. Picking this way, you take just what you need and no more. While gathering your wild salad it pays to simply spray or splash a little fresh water from a plastic bottle onto your leaves to avoid your salad wilting.

How to prepare

Wash your salad thoroughly in a sink full of cold tap water by gently plunging the leaves several times and finally rinsing them in a colander under a running cold tap. Ideally, you should serve your salad as soon as possible after picking.

How to cook/use

Try each variety individually to enable you to make a positive identification and taste test. You can then experiment with your personal favourites and design your own perfect salad.

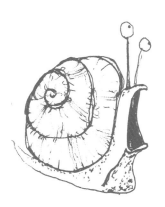

ALEXANDERS Smyrnium olusatrum

Picking season: January to June

Alexanders are indigenous to the Mediterranean and were allegedly brought here by the Romans; it's a fairly intrusive weed found growing along country lanes and roadside verges – especially along the south coast. The plant would have been used just as we use celery today. The alexander is equally succulent but has a flavour all its own – aromatic, pungent and unlike anything else you may have tasted.

How to recognise

Growing just like a ground covering bush of celery, the dense vivid green foliage can be found growing as early as January. By parting the ground covering leaf foliage with both hands you'll reveal fat celery-like stems that peel just like celery but aren't so stringy. Once peeled, the soft aromatic flesh can be eaten raw or cooked. The foliage is a useful addition to any soup or stews and can be added sparingly to salad. Use only the youngest and most tender leaves as the older ones, having lost their bright green colour, are past their sell by date and bitter. The alexander belongs to the carrot family (*umbelliferae*).

Be warned – great care should be taken not to mistake this edible plant for the very poisonous lookalike Hemlock.

Where to find

Alexanders are not very common except near the sea where they can be found in abundance growing particularly well along verges, hedgerows and old boundary earthwork banks. The large pinnate fleshy leaves suffer badly from windburn after winter gales so sheltered sunny south-facing aspects always yield the best harvest.

"You'll either love it or hate it, but believe me, the first tender shoots are well worth a try."

How to prepare

The stems should be cut as close to the ground as possible, the lower half of the alexander stem is by far the most tasty and succulent, the longer the stems the tougher and less palatable they become. Wash the stems thoroughly and peel the same way as you would celery, wash the prepared stems along with the young leaves in a colander under cold running tap water, drain and pat dry.

How to cook/use

This aromatic weed can be a little overwhelming when used on its own so blanching the young peeled stems and bright green young foliage twice in fresh boiling water will remove the bitterness. Using these sparingly in soup and stews adds an interesting new flavour. Young budding flower heads can be dipped in light batter and made into fritters and late in the summer after they've finished flowering the large black seeds can be gathered and mixed with peppercorns in a grinder.

LIME (ALSO CALLED LINDEN)
Tilia family

Picking season: April to July
Extra equipment: none

Throughout the UK majestic lime tree avenues grace some of our most glorious parks, grand country houses and royal palaces. The lime, or linden tree can grow to more than one hundred feet tall and, although not classed as wild or native, this handsome deciduous tree has been widely planted. The first leaves to open in early spring are a must to try; they're vivid green and as soft and delicate as cling film. They make a fantastic substitute for lettuce and are a great base for any spring salad.

How to recognise

The leaf of the lime tree is heart shaped with a serrated edge and bright green veins on the underside. As the tree prepares to bloom during early May, long, pale-green, leafy bracts appear with clusters of tiny flower buds dangling beneath; the buds take forever to swell. By early June, clusters of four or more petit pois-sized flower buds begin to burst open. In late June and early July the trees are in bloom and fill the morning air with a honey sweet scent and if you listen carefully you'll hear a symphony of bees collecting nectar and politely redistributing pollen.

Where to find

Parkland is probably your best bet to start looking. Over the years, the handsome lime tree has been extensively used as a commemorative tree planted by dignitaries. You may be lucky and even find a plaque to really give the game away.

Collecting tips

Only pick the small and freshly opened leaves that are completely soft to the touch and as the trees are usually pretty massive, only pick the odd leaf from individual branches around the tree. Once the tree is in full bloom, pick the flowering stem along with the bract; six to ten flowering heads will make a delicious and calming infusion similar to chamomile. In France, the flower heads are picked and dried and sold at markets as *tilleul*.

How to prepare

The freshly picked leaves should be thoroughly washed by placing them in a colander and rinsed under a running tap; dry the leaves in a salad spinner or pat them dry with a clean kitchen roll before using. If making an infusion, the freshly picked flowers can be used straight from the tree. Use a fine sieve if you don't like the bits.

How to cook/use

As soon as the first leaves are beginning to unfold in early spring, they are bursting with crisp, spring-fresh flavour. They make an excellent addition to any hedgerow salad bowl and also taste great in a sandwich. I like them in a crusty baguette with mild mature Cheddar. The flowers, used fresh or dried, make excellent tea or tisane helping to aid sleep, soothe nerves, give relief to digestion and act as a decongestant when suffering from chesty coughs and colds. For me, a lime flower infusion makes a refreshing and delicious drink to usher in the spring.

"A lazy walk in the park is a perfect way to visit the greengrocer."

SORREL Rumex acetosa

Picking season: February to mid-October
Equipment: basket or carrier bag, colander, spray bottle for water
Safety: always obtain permission from landowners and don't pick in polluted areas such as roadside verges.

Sorrel is lemony sharp. The little leaves taste of green-apple skin but their sour taste should never be underrated. It is a common and widespread plant usually found growing along roadside verges but like all foraged plants it's best to pick away from polluted and high traffic areas. To quench thirst when out walking, simply chew on a couple of sorrel leaves, the tangy freshness will cause you to salivate and it's really quite refreshing.

How to recognise

Sorrel plants can grow up to two feet tall with small insignificant red and green flowers that bloom from May onwards but it's the leaves that make it easy to identify, they resemble an arrowhead with two pointed ears that grow around the stem of the plant. When you've made a positive identification the next step is simple – have a nibble. You'll be hit with a delicious and unmistakeable sharpness caused by a concentration of oxalic acid. It's quite safe so long as you don't consume it in large quantities or too often.

Where to find

Sorrel can be found growing almost anywhere, especially where the ground has never been disturbed by heavy machinery such as a farmer's plough. Un-grazed meadows and common land are ideal places to look for sorrel and once you've got your eye in you'll find it everywhere.

Collecting tips

Hold the leaves at the base of the stem and carefully pick them off so as not to damage the plant. Always try to select the youngest, most tender leaves – older leaves can get a bit woody. The young leaves always look fresh and are less likely to have insect damage.

"Sorrel makes a zesty vinegar that's perfect for dressings and sauces."

How to prepare

Place the sorrel leaves in a colander and wash them thoroughly under a running tap, dry them with a salad spinner or simply pat them dry with some kitchen roll and the tangy leaves are ready for use.

How to cook/use

Sorrel makes an excellent addition to a spring salad and is readily available for picking as early as February. As the plant develops, the larger leaves can be made into a tangy soup or even sautéed and then blended into a bright green sauce that goes nicely with poached or pan-fried fish.

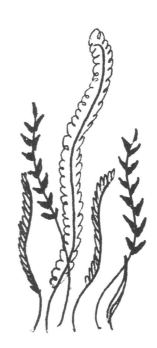

WILD GARLIC (RAMSONS) Allium ursinum

Picking season: foliage – April to June; flowers – May to June; seeds – June to July; seeds – December to January (bulbs only with landowner's permission)
Extra equipment: nimble fingers

This succulent beauty is widespread throughout the British Isles. The whole plant is edible, including the leaves, flowers, the small oval-shaped bulbs and even the seeds before they harden and turn black.

Wild garlic was possibly brought here by the Romans who most certainly used the plant for its culinary qualities as well as its medicinal powers. It's also common throughout Europe and known by a variety of different names including: wood garlic, wild leeks, broad-leafed garlic, buckrams and even bear garlic. The latter comes from the fact that bears just can't get enough of it and when the foliage is gone they'll dig like mad to get at the bulbs. Don't be too concerned, in all my years foraging I've never come across a bear munching away but unlike bears, we can't dig any wild plants without the landowner's permission.

How to recognise

Most people, quite literally, stumble across wild garlic whilst taking a woodland walk in early spring. This unmistakable plant can easily be identified from the aroma that fills the air when simply walking on them.

The pointed spear-shaped, broad, bright green leaves are delicate to the touch and have many parallel veins. They're one of the first signs of life to appear from the naked forest floor after the long cold winter months. Beds of wild garlic can cover large areas. The milder the winter, the earlier the plant can be found. Early tender leaves have a matt waxy coating, are lime green in colour and with a bit of sunshine, reach maturity in just a couple weeks. Toward the end of March, or in early April, the carpet of green foliage sends up spindly flower budding stems with a typical onion-like bud wrapped in a thin, green papery bract. As the buds swell, the bracts split open to produce a profusion of pretty white clusters of star-shaped flowers.

As summer progresses, overhead foliage blocks the sun and the garlic carpets begin to wilt away but the flower stems remain, standing proud with the flowers now replaced by small, three-lobed green fruit. The plant's job to reproduce is almost complete. As the fruit ripens it swells, bursting to reveal three small black seeds to ensure next year's heady aromatic crop. Gather a few seeds in a dry brown paper bag to disperse in a shaded border or corner of your own garden but be warned – it is a prolific grower and once started you'll never again be without it and if you're like me, that's no bad thing!

A word of warning - wild garlic is a member of the lily family and you must take care not to mistake it with the toxic and poisonous lily-of-the-valley. The lily's stem is purple and the garlic's is completely white. A good indicator is that when crushed the leaves smell strongly of garlic. If they don't or you're not sure don't eat them.

Where to find

Wild garlic's preferred habitat is along the edges of damp hedgerows or beneath the shady canopy of deciduous woods. The early shoots benefit from the spring sunshine that warms the forest floor before the leafy canopy unfurls. It normally grows as a carpet, covering large areas of damp ground and forest floors particularly where streams have overflowed during winter rainstorms. During a particularly mild winter and when the water has subsided, the small

pointed shoots can be found bursting to life from as early as the second or third week of January while harsher winters will keep you waiting another month or so. Mother Nature always likes a bit of warm weather.

Collecting tips

My ideal picking area is, in fact, alongside a small stream where the garlic will be so abundant that gathering a couple of good handfuls does no harm whatsoever. Never pick an area completely bald - simply pick a few of the freshest looking leaves from different spots as you carefully make your way through your garlicky carpet. The broad, bright-green leaves will make picking a feed quick and easy. Locate the stem of the individual leaves between your thumb and finger; guide your finger down to the base of the stem as close to the ground as possible and ease the leaf out of the ground with a gentle tug. Picking the leaves this way will also retrieve as much of the almost forced, white crisp stem as possible. Place the freshly picked leaves in a uniform way in your waiting basket and splash or spray a little clean fresh water over them to avoid them wilting too quickly. On your return home, place them in a jug of cold tap water as you would a bunch of flowers. This will help to keep them crisp and fresh, and as with all greens or vegetables, use as soon as possible after picking.

How to prepare

Simply rinse the leaves and stems of wild garlic under a running tap as you would spinach. Then, either shake the leaves to remove excess water and pat them dry with some kitchen roll or spin them in a salad spinner. Use them whole or chopped.

How to cook/use

For garlic lovers out there getting to know the wild stuff really is an absolute must. Use wild garlic in place of cultivated or home grown varieties in any recipe. As with most wild herbs the strength of flavour is greatly reduced during the cooking process, so if you're cautious about garlic give this one a try. As an added bonus wild garlic doesn't leave a lingering aftertaste or odour, so munch away. A few chopped leaves added to any dish will infuse a mild garlic flavour. It also makes a great addition to pesto.

"As for me, there's nothing better than wild garlic soup to signal that spring has truly sprung."

FORAGER'S BUTTER

Yield 300 g

250 g butter, softened

petals of 2 dandelion flowers

petals of 2 daisies

a small handful of wild sorrel,
    wild garlic & yarrow

a small handful of nettles,
    blanched & chopped

zest of ½ a lemon

salt & pepper

Break and roughly chop the foraged leaves, mix them into the butter and season to taste.

Divide into 4 quarters and spoon each onto a sheet of cling film and roll into tight rolls. Keep in the fridge until ready to use.

"Flavouring and seasoning butter is a really fun thing to do. You rarely need to look further than your own garden to find great ingredients and it looks great on a plate next to slices of warm sourdough right out of the oven."

ELDER Sambucus nigra

Picking season: May to September

Elder is very common and can be found just about anywhere in the UK. It's a deciduous shrub cum tree. During the winter months the twisted, gnarled branches and bark look completely incapable of ever producing the sweet tasting blossoms that begin to appear in May.

When crushed and added to water, the fresh leaves make a very useful, environmentally friendly, green herbal insecticide. In years gone by, the bridles of working farm animals were adorned with sprays of elder to keep away troublesome flies. Hang a few sprigs of leaf foliage in your henhouse and your chickens will be happy girls, as flies really can't stand the acrid smell. Don't let that smell put you off though.

How to identify

The elder grows up to ten metres high but usually the smaller, younger shrubs produce the best and easiest pickings. The fast growing, fresh spring growth starts life very green with the bark only turning brown as the fruit ripens in the autumn. Elder has pinnate leaves, meaning each stem has three to six or even more individual leaves, each leaf is oval with a pointed end and slightly serrated edge. The fresh green, spring growth produces miniature flower budding heads. As they slowly swell, the tiny buds turn creamy-white then bloom into dense flat-topped clusters that can have an almost sickly sweet smell. Following the flower, the green berries swell to the size of small petit pois and ripen during September then turn almost black and look highly polished.

Where to find

Elder can be found growing just about anywhere from hedgerows to forests, fields, parks, gardens and even wasteland. Just keep your eyes peeled and once you know it you'll see it everywhere.

"The flavour and bouquet of the elder's freshly opened flowers is, I assure you, second to none."

Collecting tips

Always try and pick flowering heads of elder when the weather has been fair for a few days as fresh rainfall washes away the sweet nectar. Gather only the flowers that are just barely beginning to open. The stems snap away easily but before picking, always give each one a small shake as any flower head that has petals falling is past its sell by date and should be left to form into fruiting berries and it always helps to dislodge any unwelcome guests. Early flowering heads are usually bug free although some shrubs can become infested with minute black fly that form black clusters on the stems just below the flowering heads – leave these for the bugs, insects and birds; there's more than enough to go around!

How to prepare

Take extra time and care when gathering elderflowers. It's vital that you never wash them, as water will flush away the sweet and delicious nectar that gives that amazing elder flavour. All good recipes will tell you to strain through a muslin cloth anyway so you have nothing to fear. Using kitchen scissors cut the individual flower heads away removing as much of the green stems as possible – preparation done.

How to cook/use

Elderflower cordial is one of those *must try* recipes. It's so delicious. Simply combine sugar, water, lemon and elderflowers. You can get adventurous and try elder champagne and the delicate floral twang of elderflower syrup makes a great change to honey. Also, adding a few flowering heads when warming the cream mixture for panna cotta is another mind-blower. *So go on, get in there!*

COMFREY Symphytum officinale

Picking season: May to September

When venturing out for a walk in early spring, always make certain to stuff a carrier bag or two in your pocket along with a good sharp penknife as the young tender shoots of the comfrey plant make an interesting and tasty vegetable.

Where to find

Comfrey is a perennial plant and is common, especially where the soil remains moist throughout the year. Riverbanks, lakes, ponds and even springs are always good places to keep your eyes peeled. As the plant matures, the large hairy leaves make identification easy.

Collecting tips

When you've found and positively identified your comfrey plants, the tastiest and best part to pick is the fresh growth at the tallest part of each stem. Take cuttings about a finger-length from the very end of shoots of leaves and flower budding heads, where the leaves are still unfurling and the flower buds are still tightly closed. Nipping off these end shoots has no ill effect on the plant as it simply sends out more.

"Gathering comfrey is a good, safe bet especially if you've just caught the wild food bug."

How to recognise

Comfrey is easily identifiable before flowering by its rather large Zulu spear-shaped leaves, the underside of which is extremely hairy and almost prickly to touch. The leaves are similar in shape to that of a dock leaf, though a paler green in colour, but it really is the hairs on the underside of the leaves that gives the comfrey away. I hasten to add that the prickliness vanishes completely when cooked. Once in bloom, the plant is unmistakable with its clusters of bell-shaped flowers varying in colour from creamy white and pink to purple. The flowers seem insignificant, though on closer inspection they reveal their beauty. Bees, bugs and butterflies alike love to feed on their sweet nectar and I can't say I blame them.

How to prepare

Rinse under a running cold tap, shake off excess water and prepare in the same way you would spinach.

How to cook/use

If you're into spicy cuisine the young fleshy stems have the consistency and similar flavour to okra or lady's fingers and make a great addition to any curry dish. Sautéed comfrey with onions and potato also makes an interesting change from cabbage when cooking bubble & squeak and they also make great fritters as a starter or delicious side dish.

TEMPURA ELDER & COMFREY FLOWER FRITTERS

Serves 4 as a starter
Equipment: deep-fryer, slotted spoon

12 comfrey & elderflower heads (budding but not blooming)

100 g corn flour

150 g plain flour

10 g baking powder

enough iced Perrier or soda water to make batter that should just coat your finger

1½ - 3 litres rapeseed oil for deep-frying

salt & pepper

To make the tempura mix together the flours and baking powder then gently add the iced liquid stirring only enough to just mix. The batter should be lumpy. Don't be tempted to over stir.

Preheat oil in a deep-fryer to 180°C. Dip the elderflower and comfrey heads into the batter and deep-fry until golden. Remove with a slotted spoon and drain on kitchen paper. Season to taste and serve hot.

"These are delightful bursts of foraged flavour. The tempura captures the freshness. They taste a bit like really intense sprouting broccoli. I love them!"

FENNEL Foeniculum vulgare

Picking season: May to mid-October

For me, the first sight of bright green and copper feathery fennel fronds makes me want to jump in a boat and catch a sea bass or two, or even go looking for an early sea trout returning to the estuary.

Fennel has been widely used through the ages. It was cultivated by the Romans and used as a vegetable and potherb. This attractive and fragrant plant with its pretty, almost lacy foliage was even used as an attractive garnish at banquet tables.

It also has a medicinal and cosmetic history for a variety of ailments. An infusion of fennel was said to be good for the memory and smooth away wrinkles. It was even used as a miracle cure for obesity, as well as helping to ward off evil. Powerful stuff!

How to recognise

Fennel is fairly widespread in the UK and easily identifiable by the unfurling delicate fern-like, juicy, young shoots. The leaves are more like a mass of soft spiky prickles. Crushing a few tips between your fingers will fill your nostrils with a sweet aniseed aroma and when mature, this tall handsome plant has small clusters or 'umbels' of tiny yellow flowers and stands out amongst other wayside plants as it gently sways in summer breeze. Full-grown plants can, and do, grow up to three or even four feet tall.

Where to find

Fennel is a prolific weed and will naturalise in almost any type of soil and just about anywhere from hedgerows to wasteland. In fact, the poorer the soil the happier the plant seems to be. It especially likes busy locations where the seeds can be dispersed by constant motion. Sowing a few wild seeds in or around your own garden will give you pretty foliage with the added bonus of having a great many culinary uses in your kitchen. Be sure to weed out the inevitable surplus of seedlings that will overrun your garden; the very youngest and smallest seedlings can be used whole, roots and all, as an addition to a wild spring salad and are truly scrumptious with their tender twang of anise.

"For me, this astonishing, versatile and fragrant plant simply shouts 'go catch and cook a fish."

Collecting tips

It's best to use a sharp knife to cut the feathery fronds quite close to the plant stem. All parts of the plant are edible, however, the woody stems are too chewy and the bulb lacks any flavour whatsoever and is too small to bother with. The large fennel bulbs obtainable in garden centres and supermarkets are a cultivated variety and are called '*Florence fennel*'. These larger varieties can be easily grown. The leaves are so fine that they do not dry very well but, for winter use, it is possible to collect the seeds at the end of the plant's growing season around mid-October.

How to prepare

Wash your fennel fronds one at a time under a cold running tap and shake off any excess water. Quickly spin them in a salad spinner or carefully pat dry with clean kitchen roll. Be careful not to bruise them, as this will release the all-important flavour.

How to cook/use

Used sparingly the mild aniseed flavour also makes a delicious addition to any wild salad and fennel tea infusion is refreshing and tasty. Try using a few fennel leaves in the same way you would mint. *Fennelled peas! Yeah – try it!*

If you get the timing just right, when the flowers are nearly finished but not yet gone to seed you can collect the pollen by shaking it into plastic bags. It makes an amazing seasoning.

GRILLED MACKEREL
WITH WILD FENNEL & COLUMBINE

Serves 4

4 whole mackerel, cleaned (*see page* 13)

2 *A Pinch of Salt* pancetta rashers, chopped
  into lardons

a large bunch of wild fennel fronds & stalks,
  chopped

1 shallot, finely chopped

a splash of rapeseed oil

a generous squeeze of lemon

a handful of columbine petals
  (or other edible flower)

salt & pepper

Once the mackerel is cleaned, dry with kitchen roll and season the flesh inside with a pinch of salt.

Heat a dash of rapeseed oil in a frying pan to smoking hot, add the lardons and cook until crisp. Remove the lardons and set aside then carefully add the mackerel making sure that the pan remains very hot. Cook for 1 to 2 minutes, depending on the thickness of the fish. Once the skin is crisp and golden, add a squeeze of lemon juice, turn the fish over and remove from the heat, leaving the mackerel in the pan to cook through, for 30 seconds to 1 minute.

Remove the fish from the pan and place the pan back on medium heat. Add the lardons, shallot, half the fennel stalks and fronds and sauté until just soft.

Lightly season the remaining fennel stalks and fronds and columbine petals (or other available edible flowers) with a squeeze of lemon, salt and pepper.

To serve, place the fish in the centre of plates, ladle on the lardons and fennel mixture with juices and dress with the fennel salad.

*"Mackerel has intensely rich, creamy flesh.
The strong flavour makes it a perfect fish for grilling
and a perfect partner for the freshness and crunch of the fennel."*

STINGING NETTLE Urtica dioica

Picking season: March to October
Extra equipment: sturdy garden gloves & long sleeves

Stinging nettle is probably the most common and almost
certainly, most unpopular wild edible plant. We usually think
of them as simply irritating – and they are, quite literally.
They have a nasty habit of releasing formic acid through
zillions of tiny stinging hairs and our soft pink skin hates
it. Don't let this put you off though, both the hairiness and
stinging ability completely vanish when cooked.

As children, we made great entertainment out of stinging
nettle fights. Bare legs beneath short trouser uniforms were
always the target. It seemed like fun at the time but we
always made certain there were plenty of dock or ribwort
leaves to hand to rub into our wounds to ease the tingling
effect of the nettles. Happy days!

How to identify

Nettle leaves are oval with a pointed end and coarsely
toothed edges. The whole plant is one big hairy stinger
including the stem and the underside of the leaves. It can
grow to over a metre tall and when in full bloom will have
bunches of insignificant dark green to purple flower clusters.
By the time the plant is in flower it'll be too woody to eat so
best left to pester someone else.

Where to find

Stinging nettles can colonise large areas remarkably
quickly. They love freshly loosened soil such as roadside
ditches. I don't know how they do it but the nettles always
find their way into your vegetable plot and flower borders
and even weeding out these small plants will make your
fingertips tingle but it also means you don't have to go far
to collect a feed.

Collecting tips

Only gather stinging nettles for culinary use as far from any
roadside verge and busy footpath as possible.

Gathering a feed of nettle tips after a mild winter can begin
from early March. Unless you fancy numb fingertips for
the day, wear a pair of gardening gloves and use sharp
scissors to simply snip off the fresh budding tips. The small
fresh shoot ends with the leaves still unfurling are the most
succulent and full of goodness and flavour.

How to prepare

Place your freshly cut nettle tips in a colander and wash them thoroughly under a cold running tap, spin them dry in a salad spinner or pat them dry with a clean kitchen roll before use. If you fancy trying nettle tips in a spring salad, simply blanch them and allow them to cool before use.

How to cook/use

Nettles are best when lightly blanched and added to spring salads. I like to sauté them with cooked cold potatoes and chopped onion or wild garlic to make a delicious bubble and squeak. It's a great accompaniment to any meal. They're also great when cooked with potatoes and onions and blended into soup with a swirl of cream and a sprinkling of crusty garlic croutons.

"Nettles are not only quite delicious, but are also very good for you. They contain a multitude of nutritional properties including vitamin C and are rich in iron, calcium and magnesium."

BUTTERED
BEEFSTEAK MUSHROOMS
WITH WILD NETTLE SALSA VERDE

Serves 4 as a starter or snack

4 large beefsteak mushrooms

splash of rapeseed oil

a knob of butter

salt & pepper

For the wild nettle salsa verde

2 thick slices of bread, diced

8 tbsp olive oil

2 large handfuls of nettle leaves
    (tips only), blanched

2 tbsp capers

4 garlic cloves

4 anchovies

6 cornichons

3 tbsp lemon juice

2 large handfuls of parsley, chiffonade

salt & black pepper

For the salsa verde, soak the diced bread in olive oil for 15 minutes then place in a blender with the nettle tips, capers, garlic, anchovies and cornichons, blending until well combined. Add the lemon juice and chopped parsley and season to taste.

For the beefsteak mushrooms, cut the mushrooms into thick slices. Coat a pan with rapeseed oil and heat to medium-high heat. Sear the mushrooms on both sides then add a knob of butter, nappe to finish and season to taste.

To serve place the mushrooms in the centre of the plates, top with a generous amount of salsa verde and garnish with a handful of wild salad.

(As a top tip, only season mushrooms after they've been cooked, you'll leech the moisture out of them and make them tough and flavourless.)

"Only use young beefsteak mushrooms as the mature ones get pretty tough."

YARROW
Achillea millefolium

Picking season: April to November
Extra equipment: nimble fingers

If you're not already familiar, you've probably seen this common wayside plant no matter where you live in the UK. Its foliage and flowers have been used to make curative infusions through the ages and was said to aid the symptoms of colds, headaches and flu. I personally cannot vouch for any such remedy.

How to recognise

Yarrow leaves or *fronds* are silvery dark green, fern-like and look a bit like carrot tops or fennel fronds. When in full bloom, the tight clusters of white to pinkish purple flowers make positive identification easy.

Where to find

Yarrow can be found growing almost anywhere and thrives where the grass hasn't been grazed by animals or cut by machinery, having said that, if your lawn isn't entirely weed free as mine certainly isn't, yarrow can also be found as a ground covering plant. I even mow around small patches to allow it to flower. Once you've identified yarrow, especially when the plant is in full bloom, you'll start spotting it in all manner of places but stick to good foraging rules and avoid gathering from the roadside and other heavily travelled byways.

"Yarrow tea is delicious, refreshing and one of those tastes that smiles with countryside beauty."

Collecting tips

Simply nip the feathery leaf fronds from the quite woody stem of any mature plant and they are ready to use. Drying the yarrow fronds will intensify the flavour, however, the drying process will turn the fine and delicate leaves to almost dust. If you prefer a stronger brew, it is better to simply add twice as many fresh fronds to your infusion. The fresh leaves can be found almost throughout the year; fresh is best.

How to prepare

I only gather yarrow from places where I'm happy it's been washed sufficiently by fresh rainfall but feel free to rinse yours under a running tap if you so desire - preparation done!

How to cook/use

For me, yarrow tea is without a doubt up there with mint and chamomile and the leaves and flowers can be used in the same way, fresh or dried. An infusion takes anywhere from two to six fern-like leaves per cup. Try your first infusion au naturel then decide if you want a slice of lemon or drizzle of honey. Ahhh. Zzzz.

YARROW TEA

Yield: as much as you like
Equipment: heatproof jug, fine sieve

a handful of yarrow ferns

1 lemon, sliced

honey to taste

water

Wash the yarrow leaves under a running tap and put them in a heatproof jug, pour over the freshly boiled water, allow to stand for ten minutes or so and strain to serve. Try it with or without lemon and honey.

"This is great served hot on a frosty day and equally great served in summer over ice with honey."

wild pesto

Contents

BUTTER IN A JAR

CLAM & COCKLE CHOWDER

COURT BOUILLON

CRAB APPLE JELLY

MAYONNAISE

PASTA

PICKLING LIQUOR

SALTS

SIMPLE SYRUP

SORREL VINEGAR

SOURDOUGH BREAD

WILD GARLIC PESTO

WILD MUSHROOM &

WILD GARLIC RISOTTO

Basics & extras

BASICS & EXTRAS

Throughout the book Garry has added his ideas about how to he likes to dish up his favourite foraged fare and there are a few extra recipes you need to complete James' dishes so we've added them here.

BUTTER IN A JAR

This is a fun and easy way to make the butter for James' forager's butter.

Equipment: 1 jar, lots of energy or kids to do the shaking

Fill a jar ¾ with whipping or heavy cream, the fresher and better quality the better. Seal tightly and start shaking. The cream goes through several stages, first aeration, soft whipped, then stiff whipped (about 5 minutes). Keep shaking and after another 5 or so minutes, the curd & whey separate. Squeeze extra whey from the curds, season and roll in cling film. Ta da!

It's great served as an amuse bouche with bread and a series of infused salt powders.

You can do the same using a whisk or faster using a hand mixer on high speed - you merely keep going past the whipped cream stage. Of course use the buttermilk whey for soda bread or something.

CLAM & COCKLE CHOWDER

This is a classic American clam chowder with a taste of the English sea.

Serves 4

1 kg live clams or cockles in the shell

25 g butter

100 g piece of rindless smoked streaky bacon, cut into lardons

175 medium onion, finely chopped

1 celery stick, finely chopped

25 g plain flour

500 ml full cream milk

250 g waxy potatoes, peeled & cut into 1 cm dice (Charlotte work well)

1 fresh bay leaf

2 tomatoes, skinned, de-seeded & finely chopped

100 ml double cream

1 tbsp curly parsley, chopped

sea salt & a pinch of cayenne

Tip the clams & cockles into the sink and scrub them under running cold water to remove any traces of sand and mud. Discard any that won't close when given a tap on the side of the sink. Then put them in a pan with 50 ml water, cover and cook over a high heat for about 4 minutes, shaking the pan every now and then, until they have all opened. Tip them into a colander set over a bowl to collect the cooking liquor and leave to cool slightly. Then remove the meat and discard the shells.

Melt the butter in a pan over a medium heat. Add the bacon and fry gently until lightly golden. Add the onion and fry for a further 4 to 5 minutes, stirring now and then, until the onion is soft and just beginning to colour. Add the celery and cook for a further minute. Remove the pan from the heat, stir in the flour and then gradually stir in the milk. Return to the heat, bring to the boil and stir constantly. Add the potatoes, bay leaf and all but the last tablespoon of clam cooking liquor (this might be a bit sandy) and leave to simmer for 5 minutes, until the potatoes are tender. Stir in the cooked clams, tomatoes, cream and season to taste with salt and a pinch of cayenne. Stir in the parsley and serve hot.

COURT BOUILLON

Court bouillon is used to poach or cook foods but usually doesn't become the base for a sauce as a more complex stock would. The addition of vinegar draws the flavour of the aromats and the acidity is perfect for poaching shellfish and seafood.

Yield: approximately 5 litres

1 kg fennel, cut into small pieces

1 kg onions, peeled & cut into small pieces

1 kg carrots, peeled & cut into small pieces

1 kg leeks, cut into small pieces & washed

1 kg celery, cut into small pieces

a handful of parsley stalks

5 g thyme

2 bay leaves

10 g peppercorns

10 g fennel seeds

1 star anise

5 litres water

50 g salt

75 ml white wine vinegar

Simmer all of the ingredients except the vinegar in the water for 15 minutes. Add the vinegar and remove from the heat, pass through a fine sieve and use as required.

CRAB APPLE JELLY

When these little nugget-sized gems are ripe you'll have no trouble collecting enough of them to keep you in jam for the year.

Yield: approximately 3 litres
Equipment: large heavy-bottomed pan, jelly bag or muslin straining cloth, 6 500 ml sterilised kilner jars *(see page 15)*

4 kg crab apples, washed (you can leave the stalks on)

1 kg sugar

1 litre apple cider

juice of 1 lemon

a knob of butter

Place the apples in a heavy-bottomed pan, pour in the cider then top with just enough water to just cover the apples. Bring to the boil and simmer until the fruit is a mushy pulp, (about 30 minutes).

Pour the pulp into a jelly bag or muslin cloth, securely tie it and suspend over a clean pan and let drip overnight. Do not be tempted to squeeze the bag or it will make the juice cloudy.

The next day, measure the juice, and add sugar in the ratio of 10 parts juice to 7 sugar. Add some lemon juice to taste then bring to the boil, stirring constantly to dissolve the sugar. Keep at a rolling boil for 40 minutes, skimming off any scum and make sure the mixture doesn't boil over. Remove from the heat to test.

Chill a few small plates in the freezer. To test that the jelly has reached the setting point, put a teaspoon of jelly on one of the cold plates and leave to cool. If the jelly is ready it crinkles when pushed with your finger. If the jelly doesn't crinkle place back on the heat and boil for a further ten minutes then test again. When ready, stir in a knob of butter and remove any leftover scum.

Fill the sterilised jars to the very top, as the liquid will reduce slightly as it cools. Allow to cool then seal and keep in a cool dry place. Once opened keep refrigerated. The jelly is ready to use but will keep for several months.

MAYONNAISE

Mayonnaise is an emulsion, which is simply a mixture of two different liquids that really don't want to combine, but is so easy to make and far superior to anything bought in a jar. The type of oil will determine the richness. Use rapeseed or sunflower for light and olive for richer and peppery. This contains raw egg so must be kept refrigerated in a sealed container and used within two days.

1 egg yolk

1 tsp white wine vinegar

1 tbsp Dijon mustard

salt & freshly cracked black pepper, to taste

200 ml oil, (sunflower, rapeseed or olive)

juice of 1 lemon, add to taste

Whisk the egg yolk, vinegar, mustard, salt and pepper until smooth and the salt is dissolved. Then whisk the oil a drop at a time until the mixture begins to emulsify. Continue to add in a steady but delicate stream until thick. Add lemon juice and final seasoning to taste.

PASTA

Fresh pasta is great whether you use it immediately or dry it. The dough also freezes well so it's easy to keep a supply to hand.

Serves 4
Equipment: food processor, pasta press & drying rack, scone cutter for ravioli & tortellini

200 g strong flour (tipo '00')

9 egg yolks

5 ml olive oil

Blend the flour, egg yolks and oil together in a food processor until a dough is formed. Leave to rest in a refrigerator for 1 hour before use.

Roll on a pasta machine to desired thickness and cut into preferred shape. Hang to dry until ready to use. (If making ravioli or tortellini you may want to roll the pasta sheet to make it a bit finer.)

When ready to use, bring a pan of salted water to a rolling boil. Drop in the pasta and cook for approximately 2 minutes until just al dente. Don't overcook. Strain away the water and add to your desired sauce.

As an alternative, you can prepare in advance. Bring a pan of salted water to the boil adding a splash of olive oil. Blanch the noodles for 20 seconds then plunge into iced water then you can finish cooking by adding them to a hot sauce such as vongole with Manila clams just before serving.

PICKLING LIQUOR

Wild plants and roots lend themselves to pickling. It's also a great way to keep seasonal ingredients to hand. The pickling recipes vary through this book but here's James' standby recipe.

A few of James' favourite wild ingredients for pickling include:

Chanterelle (pictured above right)

Horseradish (see page 131)

Oxeye daisy buds (pictured above left)
   (they make a great salad seasoning when deep-fried)

Rock samphire (see page 67)

Sea purslane (see page 79)

Yield: approximately 1 medium jar
Equipment: medium sterilised kilner jar
(see page 15)

1 garlic clove, finely sliced

1 bay leaf

350 ml cider vinegar

1 tsp sugar

6 black peppercorns

1 star anise

2 allspice berries

1 tsp coriander seeds

1 tbsp fennel seeds

Clean the ingredient you're pickling thoroughly and make sure it's dry. Pack the ingredient into a sterilised jar with the bay leaf and finely sliced garlic.

In a small non-reactive pan (see page 199), gently heat the cider vinegar, sugar and spices until the sugar has dissolved and then bring to the boil for 5 minutes. Pour the hot pickling liquid over the ingredient straight into the jar. Seal tightly and leave to mature in a cool dark place for 1 month. You can store unopened for up to 6 months but once opened refrigerate and use within a week.

SALTS

Infused salts are a great way to add character and interest to your table. The possibilities are endless and the process is simple. An electric dehydrator is a useful appliance for preparing larger items such as celery, chilli and onions and more subtle flavours like rose petal and hyacinth can be used by air-drying the petals. Herbs, like rosemary are easy to dry in a microwave. It's really worth experimenting a bit to see what you like best.

Equipment: electric dehydrator, electric coffee bean grinder, mortar & pestle

There isn't really a set process or precise amounts to measure. All you need is good quality sea salt flakes or 'fleur de sel' and your preferred seasoning, then choose your method of dehydrating the ingredients (*see page* 14). Here are a few ideas:

Celery salt (*see page* 85)
Smoked salt (*see page* 61)

Laverweed salt
Laverweed, like all other seaweeds, when powdered or crushed, is flavoursome enough to use as a seasoning on its own.

To prepare the crispy laverweed (*see page* 61). Make sure it's bone dry then crush it using a mortar and pestle or simply chop it very finely with a knife. Add salt to taste.

Rosemary salt
To dehydrate rosemary sprigs, place a handful on kitchen roll in a microwave for 10 second bursts at a time checking each time until they are completely dry, then, with a pestle and mortar crush to a fine dust mix. Add salt to taste.

Wild cep salt
It's best to use an electric dehydrator to dry the mushrooms and once dried they will keep in a sterilised, airtight container for months. This is also a great seasoning on its own.

Chop the dried mushrooms into pieces small enough to fit into a coffee bean grinder then whizz into a fine dust and add to salt.

Wild garlic salt
Oven dry or dehydrate a generous handful of ramson leaves then put them in a mortar and roughly crush them with a pestle. Mix into salt and if you have a few dried flower petals pop them in as well.

SIMPLE SYRUP

Simple syrup is the foundation of many confections and cocktails. It ensures the prevention of sugar crystalising in preparation and it's easy to control the level of sweetness.

Yield: approximately 350 ml
Equipment: sterilised bottle if preserving (*see page* 15)

225 g sugar, (1 cup)
250 ml water, (1 cup)

Pour the water and sugar into a pan, bring to the boil and simmer until the sugar is completely dissolved. Remove from the heat and allow to cool completely. If preserving, pour into a sterilised sealable bottle keep in the refrigerator. It will last for up to 1 month.

SOURDOUGH BREAD

Sourdough starter is readily available and once you've made a loaf you'll never buy store bought again.

Yield: 1 loaf
Equipment: round banneton or proving basket

375 g strong white flour, plus extra for dusting

25 g sourdough starter

7.5 g salt

130 to 175 ml tepid water

olive oil for kneading

Combine the flour, starter and salt in a large mixing bowl. Add the water a splash at a time and mix with your hands to make a soft dough (you may not need all of the water).

Coat a chopping board or work surface with olive oil, then tip the dough onto it and knead the dough for 10 to 15 minutes until the dough is smooth and elastic. (Don't scrimp it's a bit of a workout but essential.)

Tip the dough into a lightly oiled bowl, cover with cling film and leave to rise in a warm place for five hours until at least doubled in size.

Tip the dough onto a lightly floured surface and knead until it's smooth, knocking the air out. Roll into a ball and dust with flour. Place the dough into a well-floured round banneton or proving basket and leave to rise for 4 to 8 hours until it has doubled in size again.

Preheat oven to 220°C and place a tray half-filled with water on the lower oven shelf.

Gently tip the risen dough onto a parchment-lined baking tray and bake for 30 minutes then reduce the heat to 200°C and bake for a further 15 to 20 minutes. You will know that it's done if you tap it and it makes a hollow sound. Allow to cool on a wire rack.

SORREL VINEGAR

This is a perfect use for wild sorrel. It mellows the vinegar so is great to use in vinaigrettes.

a handful of sorrel

white wine vinegar

Wash and dry a good handful of sorrel leaves and crush them in your hands to bruise them slightly to release the flavour. Now put them in a vinegar decanter and top up with cold white wine vinegar, seal the top with a cork, give it a quick shake and allow to infuse for 24 hours. You can keep topping it up with fresh leaves and vinegar as you use it.

WILD GARLIC PESTO

This is a lovely variation on regular pesto. It's marvelous with pasta hot or cold but it's perfect served simply on toasted sourdough bruschetta.

Yield: 1 medium-sized kilner jar
Equipment: food processor, sterilised kilner jar (see page 15)

a large bunch of wild garlic leaves, washed

a small bunch of curly parsley

60 g pine nuts, toasted

80 g Parmesan

150 ml fine extra virgin olive oil

a squeeze of lemon juice

salt & freshly cracked black pepper

Place all the ingredients except the oil in a food processor and blitz to a rough pulp then slowly pour in the olive oil until blended. Season to taste and transfer to a sterilised jar if storing. If using immediately it will keep in a sealed jar in the fridge for up to 2 weeks.

WILD MUSHROOM & WILD GARLIC RISOTTO

This is a perfect dish after a morning gathering wild mushrooms & garlic.

Serves 4

2 tbsp olive oil

1 onion, chopped

1 garlic clove, chopped

175 g Arborio rice

1 litre vegetable stock

1 tbsp olive oil

400 g wild mushrooms (whatever's in season)

100 g Parmesan, grated

a few leaves of fresh ramson, chopped

a few 3-cornered garlic flowers to garnish

salt & freshly ground black pepper

white truffle oil, for drizzling

slices of sourdough to mop up the sauce & a glass of crisp Italian chardonnay

For the risotto, heat the olive oil in a pan. Place in the onions and garlic and cook without colour. Add the rice and stir until very hot and the grains start to turn translucent. Add the stock a ladle at a time and stir continuously. Cook for 20 minutes then remove the pan from the heat and leave to stand.

To complete the risotto, heat a little olive oil in a frying pan, add the mushrooms and fry until softened then mix them through the risotto base. Stir in the Parmesan and chopped ramson. Season with salt and freshly ground black pepper.

To serve, place the risotto into the middle of four serving dishes, drizzle over a little white truffle oil and top with a few garlic flowers.

GLOSSARY

GLOSSARY OF FORAGING TERMS

Estuary

An estuary is a body of water formed where freshwater from rivers and streams flows into the ocean, mixing with the seawater. Estuaries and the lands surrounding them are places of transition from land to sea, and freshwater to saltwater. Although influenced by the tides, estuaries are protected from the full force of ocean waves, winds and storms by barriers such as reefs, fingers of land, mud or sand that surround them.

Foreshore

The part of a shore between high and low water marks or between the water and cultivated or developed land.

Gastropod

Any of numerous molluscs of the class Gastropoda, characteristically having a single, usually coiled shell or no shell at all, a ventral muscular foot, and eyes and tentacles located on a distinct head including the snails, slugs, winkles and limpets.

Molluscs

Any invertebrate of the phylum *Mollusca*, having a soft un-segmented body and often a shell, secreted by a fold of skin (the mantle). The group includes the gastropods (such as snails, winkles and limpets), bivalves (cockles, clams and mussels) and cephalopods (cuttlefish, squid and octopus)

Intertidal zone

Also known as the foreshore and seashore and sometimes referred to as the *littoral zone,* is the area that is above water at low tide and under water at high tide (in other words, the area between tide marks).

Spring & neap tides

The combined tide raising forces of the moon and sun are at their greatest effect when they are in line with the earth during a new or full moon. They have their least effect when they are approximately at right angles to each other. This happens at the first and last quarters of the moon. These variations affect the high tidal wave and hence the range of the tide (the difference in level between successive high and low waters). Shortly after full or new moon a locality will experience its highest high waters and lowest low waters of the lunar month. These are called *spring tides*.

Conversely around the time of the first and last quarters of the moon, the lowest high waters and the highest low waters of the lunar month will be experienced, at which period the tides are called *neap tides*.

GLOSSARY OF CULINARY TERMS

Blanch

To plunge foods into boiling water for a few seconds or until just softening then transferring to ice water. The process sets the color of vegetables, makes fruit easy to peel and slips the skins off nuts. The food should not cook through and a crisp texture must be preserved. Blanching also denatures enzymes that makes food spoil so is usually the first step in canning and preparing preserves.

Chiffonade

A French word meaning 'little ribbons'. In culinary terms it is a chopping technique used on herbs, leafy vegetables as well as crêpes and thin omelettes. This is accomplished by stacking leaves (or crêpes), rolling them tightly then slicing perpendicular to the roll.

'Cook without colour'

To cook at a lower temperature so that the food doesn't caramelise allowing water to evaporate but retaining the sugar and starch that browns the food. It is frequently used as a technique for sautéing onions, shallots and garlic as a seasoning base for meats and sauces.

Dariole moulds

Dariole is a French word that refers to a small, cylindrical mould. They are typically made from aluminium as this offers the best overall distribution of heat or cold and used for both sweet and savoury dishes.

Dredge

A cooking technique used to coat wet or moist foods with a dry ingredient prior to cooking. It is simply pulling or rolling the wet food through the dry material to provide an even coating. The technique is particularly common with breaded and deep-fried foods, such as fish and fritters.

Grilling

Has a slightly different interpretation in a variety of cultures but generally involves dry heat applied to the surface of food, commonly from below or above. It usually involves a significant amount of direct, radiant heat and tends to be used for cooking meat quickly. Grilled food is cooked on an open grill such as a gridiron (with a heat source above or below), a grill pan (similar to a frying pan but with raised ridges to mimic the wires of an open grill), or griddle (a flat plate heated from below). Grilled meat acquires a distinctive roasted aroma and flavor from a chemical process called the *Maillard Reaction* and only occurs when foods reach temperatures in excess of 155 °C.

'Knob of butter'
Approximately 1 tablespoon.

Liquid glucose
Often called glucose syrup, is a sugar sweetener used in making sweet dishes, desserts jams and ice creams. It helps to prevent the formation of sugar crystals so is particularly useful in making confectionaries and frozen desserts. It's available at all major grocery stores.

Nappe
In culinary terms, *nappe* refers to the ability of a liquid to 'coat the back of a spoon' or the act of coating a food (ie to nappe a leg of lamb with glaze).

Non-reactive pan
Pans made of materials that won't react with certain ingredients. Specifically, certain acidic foods such as tomatoes, citrus, wine, chutneys, pickles, and cranberries. An interaction can either darken the ingredient or cause a metallic taste.

Non-reactive material includes glass, plastic, stainless steel, glazed ceramic, unglazed clay, CorningWare, or non-stick (which has the metal coated.) Calphalon and Alpholon cookware have non-reactive surfaces on them. Le Creuset has a porcelain surface over the cast iron.

Reactive metals include aluminum, cast iron and copper. High quality copper pots are fine as they are usually lined with stainless steel or anodised aluminium. Aluminium foil is one of the most reactive materials in the kitchen.

Preparing shellfish
All shellfish should smell of the fresh, sweet sea. They are best prepared live and cooked when very fresh. The shells of clams, cockles and mussels should be tightly shut or should shut immediately if you tap them - when they die, they decompose quickly and may not be safe to eat, even after a short

period of time. Before cooking leave to soak in fresh cold water for 24 hours to allow them to purge any sand and grit and wash thoroughly and make sure to discard any shells that don't open after cooking.

Pickling
The process of preserving or extending the lifespan of food by either anaerobic fermentation in brine or immersion in vinegar. The procedures typically affect the food's texture and flavor. Properly done, the pH balance will drop below pH4.6, which is sufficient to kill most bacteria allowing perishable foods for extended periods.

Unlike the canning process, pickling doesn't require foods to be completely sterile before being sealed. The flavour of the end product is determined by the addition of antimicrobial herbs and spices such as mustard seed, garlic, cinnamon and cloves along with the acidity or salinity of the pickling liquor, the temperature of fermentation and the exclusion of oxygen.

Salamander
Used for browning, caramelising, glazing, grilling and toasting. They are used to finish off foods, rather than cook them. The heat or flame is generated above rather than below. The North American terminology is typically 'boiler'.

'Season to taste'
Generally means to add salt and pepper to taste but for a trained chef it means finding the perfect balance between salt, sweet, sour, heat, bitterness, acid and so forth. When preparing dishes, season throughout the process as this produces a different flavour to seasoning only at the end of preparation.

Silpat mat
Is the brand name of a silicone mat used in baking and the production of candy to

provide a non-stick surface without the use of fat or greaseproof paper.

Smokers
Cold smoking is typically used as a flavour enhancer. The item is hung then cold smoked just long enough to infuse flavour. Smokehouse temperatures for cold smoking are typically done between 20 and 30°C.

Hot smoking exposes foods to smoke and heat in a controlled environment. Like cold smoking, the item is hung first; then smoked. Although foods that have been hot smoked are often reheated or cooked, they are typically safe to eat without further cooking. Hot smoking occurs within the range of 52 to 80°C.

Sterlising jars
Jars should be made from glass and free of any chips or cracks. Preserving or canning jars are topped with a glass, plastic or metal lid, which has a rubber seal. Two-piece lids are best for canning, as they vacuum-seal when processed. To sterilise, wash jars, lids and a pair of tongs with hot, soapy water then boil the jars and lids in a large saucepan, covered with water for 15 minutes. Use tongs when handling the sterilised jars and lids. As a rule, hot preserves go into hot jars and cold preserves go into cold jars. All items used in the process of making jams, jellies and preserves must be clean. This includes any towels used, and especially your hands.

Thermometers
Meat thermometers are used to accurately measure the internal temperature of meat and the degree of 'doneness' that correlates closely with the temperature while cooking.
Sugar (or candy) thermometers are used to measure the temperature at the stage of cooking a sugar solution. It is also used for accuracy in deep-frying.

CONVERSION TABLE

Liquid measures		Solid measures		Linear measures	
15ml	½ fl oz	5g	⅛ oz	3mm	⅛ inch
20ml	¾ fl oz	10g	¼ oz	5mm	¼ inch
25ml	1 fl oz	15g	½ oz	1cm	½ inch
35ml	1¼ fl oz	20g	¾ oz	2cm	¾ inch
40ml	1½ fl oz	25g	1 oz	2.5cm	1 inch
50ml	2 fl oz	40g	1½ oz	3cm	1⅛ inch
60ml	2¼ fl oz	50g	2 oz	4cm	1½ inch
65ml	2½ fl oz	65g	2½ oz	4.5cm	1¼ inch
85ml	3 fl oz	75g	3 oz	5cm	2 inches
100ml	3½ fl oz	90g	3½ oz	6cm	2½ inches
120ml	4 fl oz	100g	4 oz (¼ lb)	7.5cm	3 inches
150ml	5 fl oz (¼ pint)	120g	4½ oz	9cm	3½ inches
175ml	6 fl oz	135g	4¾ oz	10cm	4 inches
200ml	7 fl oz	150g	5 oz	13cm	5 inches
250ml	8 fl oz	165g	5½ oz	15cm	6 inches
275ml	9 fl oz	175g	6 oz	18cm	7 inches
300ml	10 fl oz (½ pint)	185g	6½ oz	20cm	8 inches
325ml	11 fl oz	200g	7 oz	23cm	9 inches
350ml	12 fl oz	215g	7½ oz	25cm	10 inches
375ml	13 fl oz	225g	8 oz (½ lb)	28cm	11 inches
400ml	14 fl oz	250g	9 oz	30cm	12 inches (1 ft)
450ml	15 fl oz (¾ pint)	275g	10 oz		
475ml	16 fl oz	300g	11 oz		
500ml	17 fl oz	350g	12 oz (¾ lb)		
550ml	18 fl oz	375g	13 oz		
575ml	19 fl oz	400g	14 oz		
600ml	20 fl oz (1 pint)	425g	15 oz		
750ml	1¼ pints	450g	16 oz (1 lb)		
900ml	1½ pints	550g	1¼ lb		
1 ltr	1¾ pints	750g	1½ lb		
1.2 ltr	2 pints	1kg	2¼ lb		
1.25 ltr	2¼ pints	1.25kg	2½ lb		
1.5 ltr	2½ pints	1.5kg	3½ lb		
1.6 ltr	2¾ pints	1.75kg	4 lb		
1.75 ltr	3 pints	2kg	4½ lb		
2 ltr	3½ pints	2.25 g	5 lb		

Liquid measures

2.25 ltr	4 pints
2.5 ltr	4½ pints
2.75 ltr	5 pints
3.4 ltr	6 pints
3.9 ltr	7 pints
4.5 ltr	8 pints
5 ltr	9 pints

Solid measures

2.5 kg	5½ lb
2.75 kg	6 lb
3 kg	7 lb
3.5 kg	8 lb
4 kg	9 lb
4.5 kg	10 lb
5 kg	11 lb
5.5 kg	12 lb

Oven temperatures

Gas	C	C fan	F	Oven Temp
¼	110	90	225	very cool
½	120	100	250	very cool
1	140	120	275	cool or slow
2	150	130	300	cool or slow
3	160	140	325	warm
4	180	160	350	moderate
5	190	170	375	medium hot
6	200	180	400	fairly hot
7	220	200	425	hot
8	230	210	450	very hot
9	240	220	275	very hot

JAMES' PREFERRED SUPPLIERS

James works closely with a number of local farmers, food producers and suppliers. They all share a common view of responsible farming, sourcing and sustainability. Their produce is available at local farmers markets, selected stockists and online:

A Pinch of Salt, New Milton; is a curing company that produces a full charcuterie range using high quality local produce from Hampshire and the New Forest. Butcher Alan Bartlett personally hand crafts *'A Pinch of Salt' Hampshire Charcuterie* using James' recipes.

Breadport Bakery, New Milton; baker Stephan produces artisan breads and James' favourite sourdough.

Chalk Stream Foods, Romsey; farm founder Hugo provides rainbow trout from his sustainable farms fed by the spring-fed chalk streams of the Test and Itchen rivers.

Fluffetts Farm, Fordingbridge; provide free-range eggs. The farm has gained a reputation for maintaining the highest standards of food safety and bird welfare.

Howet's Hives, New Forest; James uses their set honey in many of his dishes and dressings. The hives are scattered thoughout the New Forest and near Southampton giving the honey delicious and earthy flavours of the forest.

Lyburn Cheese Farmhouse Cheesemakers, Landford near Salisbury; Mike & Judy Smales and family have been producing their award winning cheeses for generations. James uses their *Old Winchester* as an alternative to Parmesan.

T Bartlett & Sons, New Milton; Alan Bartlett has been the Golding family butcher since James was a boy so he grew up on their sausages and meats and still serves them in his restaurant.

Tatchbury Manor Farm, Winsor near Southampton; hand rears slow-growing Tamworth pigs. They also produce a range of pork pies, saveloy, haslet, bacon and ham using preservative-free methods from traditional recipes.

The Cold Pressed Oil Company, Crondall near Farnham; farmer and producer Rob makes pure extra virgin rapeseed oil that James uses as a great alternative to imported olive oil.

The Garlic Farm, Isle of Wight; nobody knows more about garlic than Colin Boswell. He and his family have continued the tradition that his mother Norah started over 40 years ago. There's no need to go to the continent when some of the finest garlic is right here at home.

The Tomato Stall, Isle of Wight; grows over 40 varieties every year. Their entire growing system is biodegradable and they even use a fleet of bumblebees and butterflies to cross-pollinate the plants in the nurseries.

These are just a few of the producers that provide the highest quality local food – we simply couldn't list them all. For further information about them or if you want to know about others go to:

Dorset Food & Drink at www.dorsetfoodanddrink.co.uk

Hamshire Fare at www.hampshirefare.co.uk

Hampshire Farmer's Market at www.hampshirefarmersmarkets.co.uk

New Forest Marque at www.newforestmarque.co.uk

Additionally, there are similar organisations that market, promote and support local farmers and food producers throughout the UK. If you're heading to a particular region it's worth looking them up.

If you want to find out more about foraging and wild food go to: www.wildcook.co.uk

INDEX

A

A Pinch of Salt 47, 105, 111
alcohol use 13
alexanders 160-1

B

Basics & extras 190
Becoming the Wildcook 16-9
beefsteak mushrooms 183
beetroot mash 119
black chanterelles (*see* horn of plenty)
black pudding 99
blackberries 146-9
    coulis 141
    sorbet 148-9
    wild 141
black-headed gull's eggs 80-5
    soft-boiled with celery salt 84-5
blackthorn (*see* sloes)
Breadport Bakery 202
brown shrimp 32-5, 75
    potted 34-5
butter 190
    forager's 169

C

celery salt 85
cep 92-5
    summer 92-5
    wild, with mushroom & potato
        scones 94-5
Chalk Stream Foods 202
chanterelle 106-6, 110-1
checking tide times 11
chestnut (*see* sweet chestnut)
    ice cream & candied 122-3
clams (*see* Manila clams)
clam & cockle chowder 190
comfrey 172-5
    tempura fritters 174-5
common cockles 48-51, 190
cockles & clams & foraged sea
    vegetables 50-1

conversion table 200-1
cooking times 14
coppa 111
court bouillon 39, 191
crab apple 116-9
    fritters 119
    jelly 191
    New Forest wood pigeon &, with
        beetroot mash 168-9
crispy laverweed 51, 61, 75

D

damsons 142-5
    jelly 144-5
dehydrating vegetables 14
distilled rose water 153
dog rose hips 150-3
    Turkish delight 152-3
Dorset Food & Drink 202

E

edible flowers 14
eggs 13
    duck 99
    scrambled 105
elder 170-1
    tempura fritters 174-5

F

fennel, wild 176-9
    grilled mackerel with, & columbine
        178-9
Fluffets Farm 202
foraged sea vegetables 51
forest floor & more, The 88-91
flower of the wood 108-9

G

garlic, wild 166-9
    breadcrumbs 43
    forager's butter 168-9
    pesto 196
    three-cornered 47, 71, 115
Gathering shellfish 26-7

girolle (*see* flower of the wood)
grey chanterelle (*see* chanterelle)

H

Hampshire Fare 202
Hampshire Farmers Market 202
hawthorn 138-141
    panna cotta with blackberries &
        coulis 140-1
hedgehog mushrooms 112-5
    & oysters on sourdough 114-5
Hedgerow harvest 126-7
horn of plenty 102-5
horseradish 128-131
    wild pickled 130-1
Howet's Hives 202
Hutson, Robin, foreword 7

L

laver (laverweed) 56-61
    crispy with smoked sea salt 60-1
lemon
    butter sauce 75
    tartar sauce 31
lime 162-3
linden (*see* lime)
Lyburn Cheese Farmhouse Cheesemakers 95
    Old Winchester 101
    Winchester 95

M

mackerel 179
malt vinegar 30
Manila clams 40-3, 191
    grilled with butter 42-3
mayonnaise 192
measurements & quantities 15, 200-1
mushrooms, wild; A bit on picking 91
    beefsteak with wild nettle salsa
        verde 182-3
    cep 92-5
    wild, with mushroom & potato
        scones 94-5
    hedgehog 112-5

& oysters on sourdough 114-5
horn of plenty 102-5
smoked salmon & scrambled eggs
    104-5
Italian, wild pickled 111
oyster 96-7
& oysters on sourdough 114-5
with *Bartlett's* black pudding & duck
    egg 98-9
risotto 196
winter chanterelle 106-111
A Pinch of Salt coppa salad with
    pickled 110-1
pickled 111, 193
mussels 71

N

New Forest Marque 202

O

On the beach 54-5
oven temperatures 15, 201
oyster mushrooms 96-101
    with *Bartlett's* black pudding & duck
      egg 98-9

P

panna cotta 141
pasta 192
penny bun (*see* cep), 119
pesto, wild garlic 196
pickling liquor 193
    chanterelle 193
    horseradish 131
    ox eye daisies 193
    rock samphire 47, 85
    sea purslane 31
pied de mouton
    (*see* mushrooms, hedgehog)
porcini (*see* cep)
positive identification 11

R

ramsons (*see* wild garlic)
razor clams 44-7
    sautéed with chorizo 46-7
risotto, wild mushroom & garlic 196
rock limpet 28-31
    devilled 30-1
roundfish, cleaning & filleting 13

S

safety 11
salsa verde, wild nettle 183
salts
    celery 85
    laverweed 194
    rosemary 194
    smoked 61
    wild cep 194
    wild garlic 194
samphire 51
    marsh 62-4
    pickled rock 66-7
    rock 65-7
scones, mushroom & potato 95
sea beet 51, 68-71, 101
    mussels in wine & garlic with, 70-1
sea kale 72-5
    & brown shrimp with lemon butter
      sauce 74-5
sea purslane 51, 76-9
    pickled 78-9
seasoning 15
shellfish
    cleaning 14
    gathering 26
simple syrup 194
sloes 132-7
    dressing 119
    gin 134-5
    gin jam 136-7
smoked salmon (*see A Pinch of Salt*) 105
smoked sea salt 61

sorrel, wild 99, 164-5
    vinegar 195
sourdough bread 195
special equipment 15
spicy chorizo 47
sterilising jars & lids 15
stinging nettle 100-1, 180-183
    buttered beefsteak mushrooms with,
      salsa verde 182-3
    pappardelle with sautéed wild
      mushrooms 100-1
    pasta 101
    purée 101
    salsa verde 183
summer cep (*see* cep)
sweet chestnut 120-3

T

T Bartlett & Sons 99, 202
Tatchbury Manor Farm 202
tempura batter 175
The Cold Pressed Oil Company 202
The Garlic Farm 202
The Tomato Stall 202
trompette de la morte
    (*see* horn of plenty)

W

when Garry met James 21
when James met Garry 23
wild salad 156-165
winkles 36-9
    cooked in court bouillon 38-9
winter chanterelle 111
    A Pinch of Salt coppa salad with,
      pickled 110-1
wood pigeon 119

Y

yarrow 184-7
    tea 186-7
yellow legs (*see* chanterelle)